OTHER NATURE

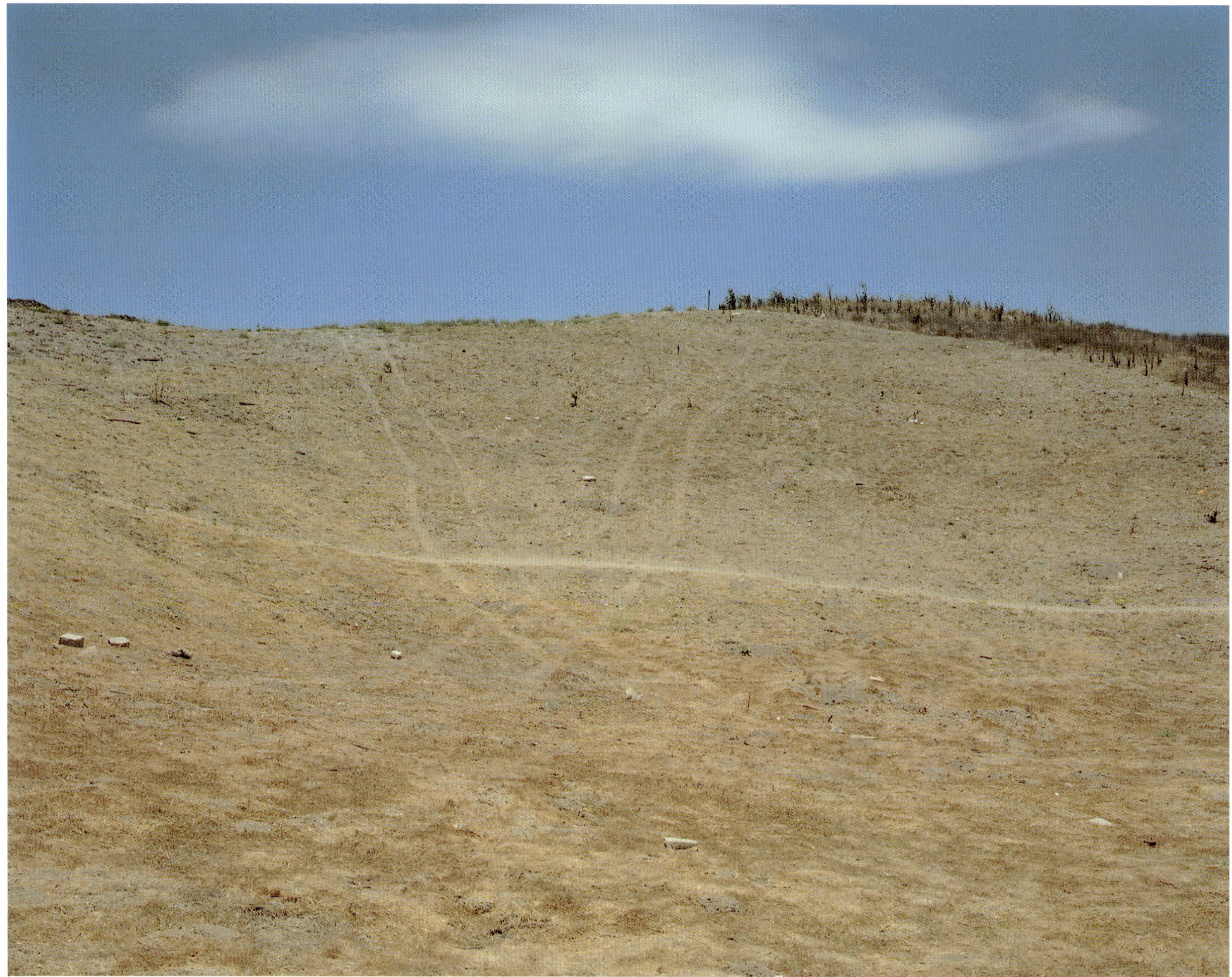

Other Nature

photographs by RON JUDE

THE ICE PLANT
Los Angeles, California

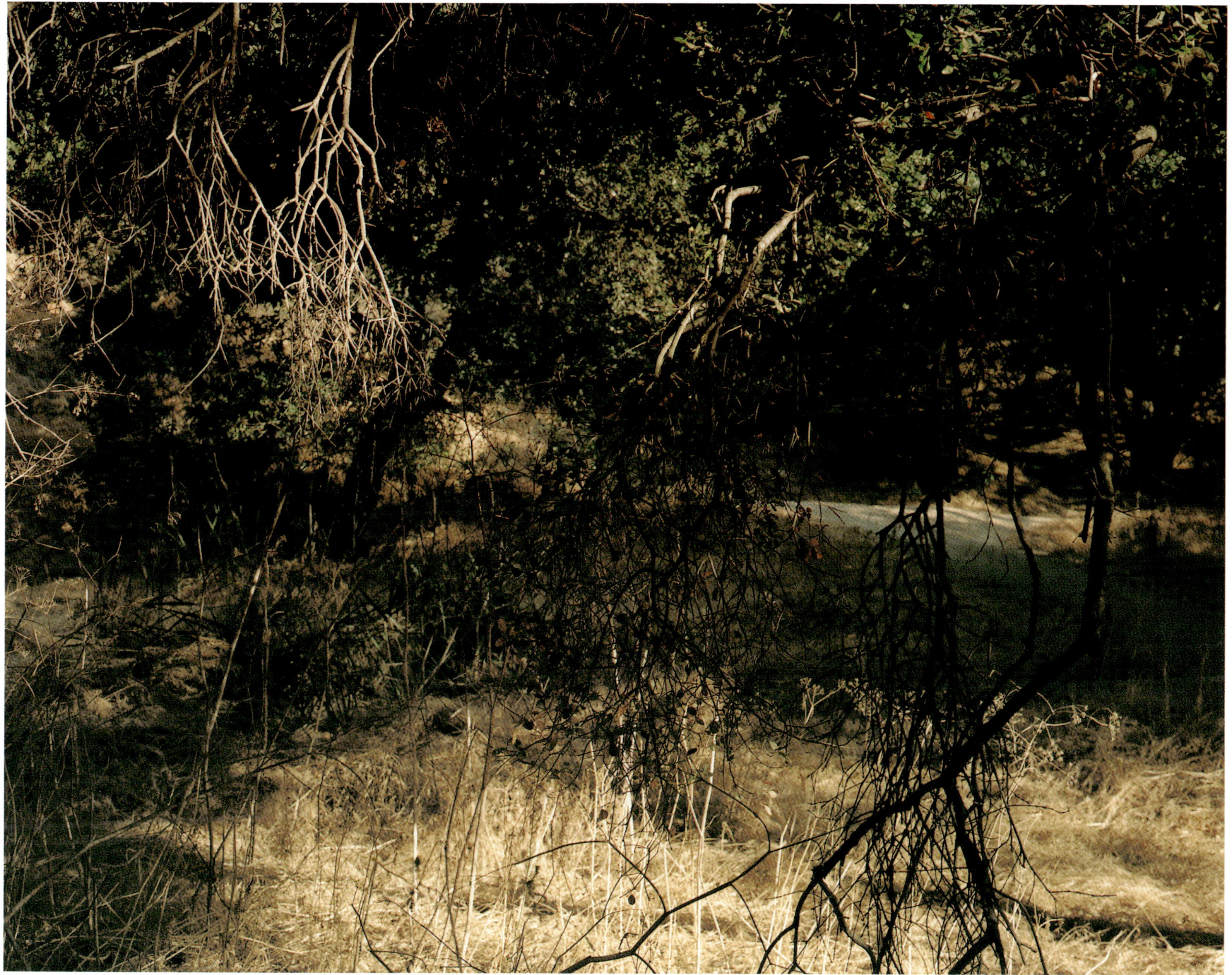

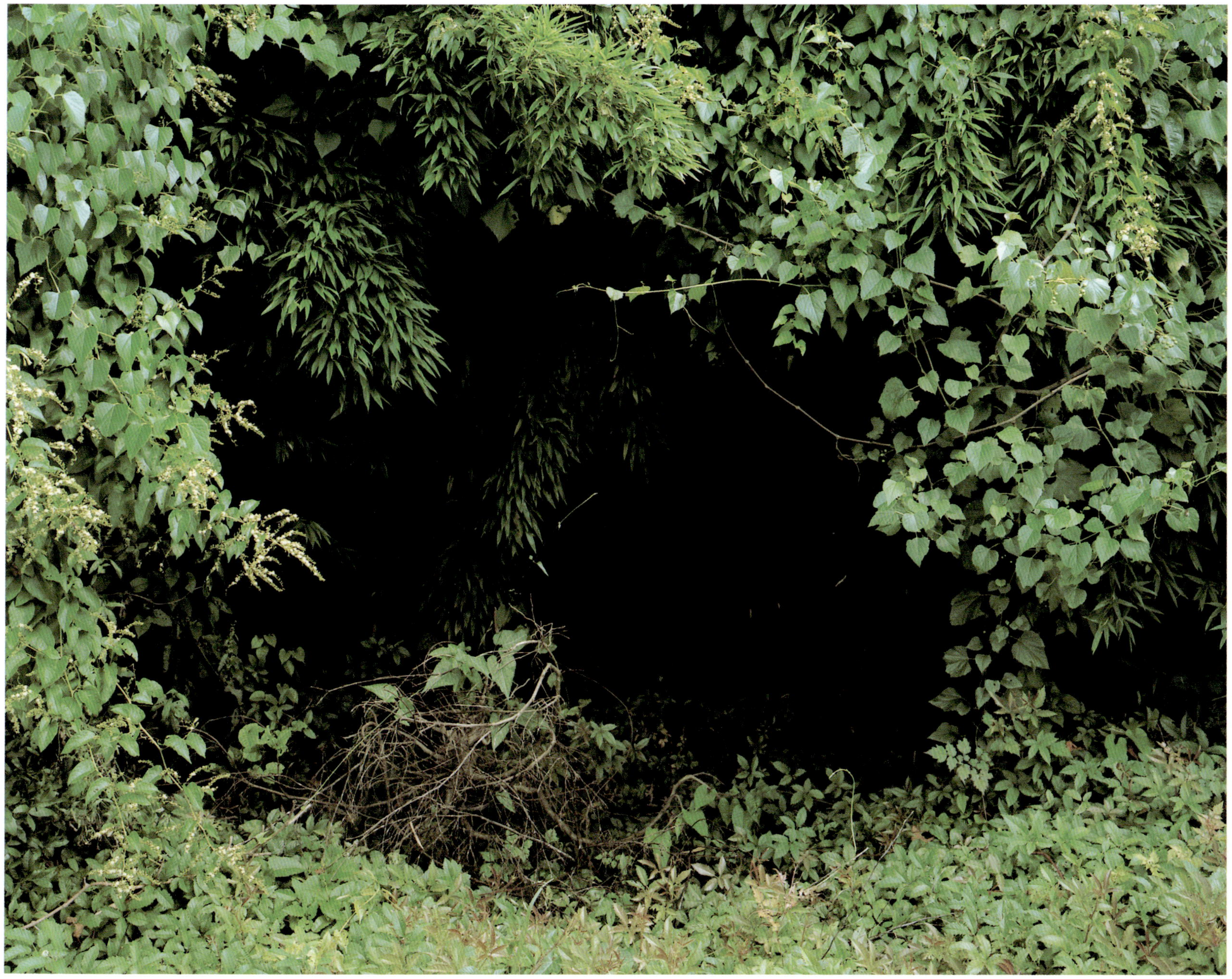

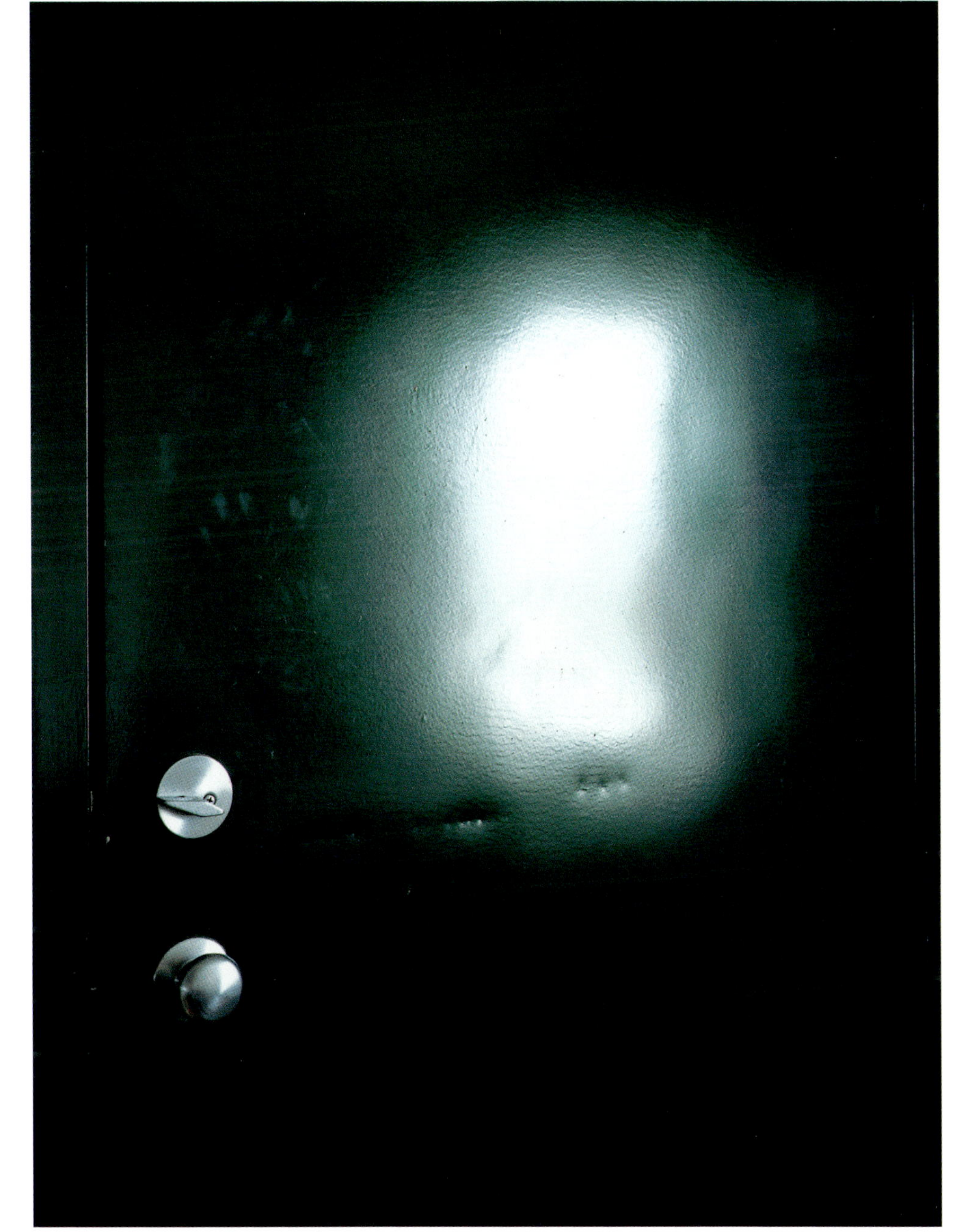

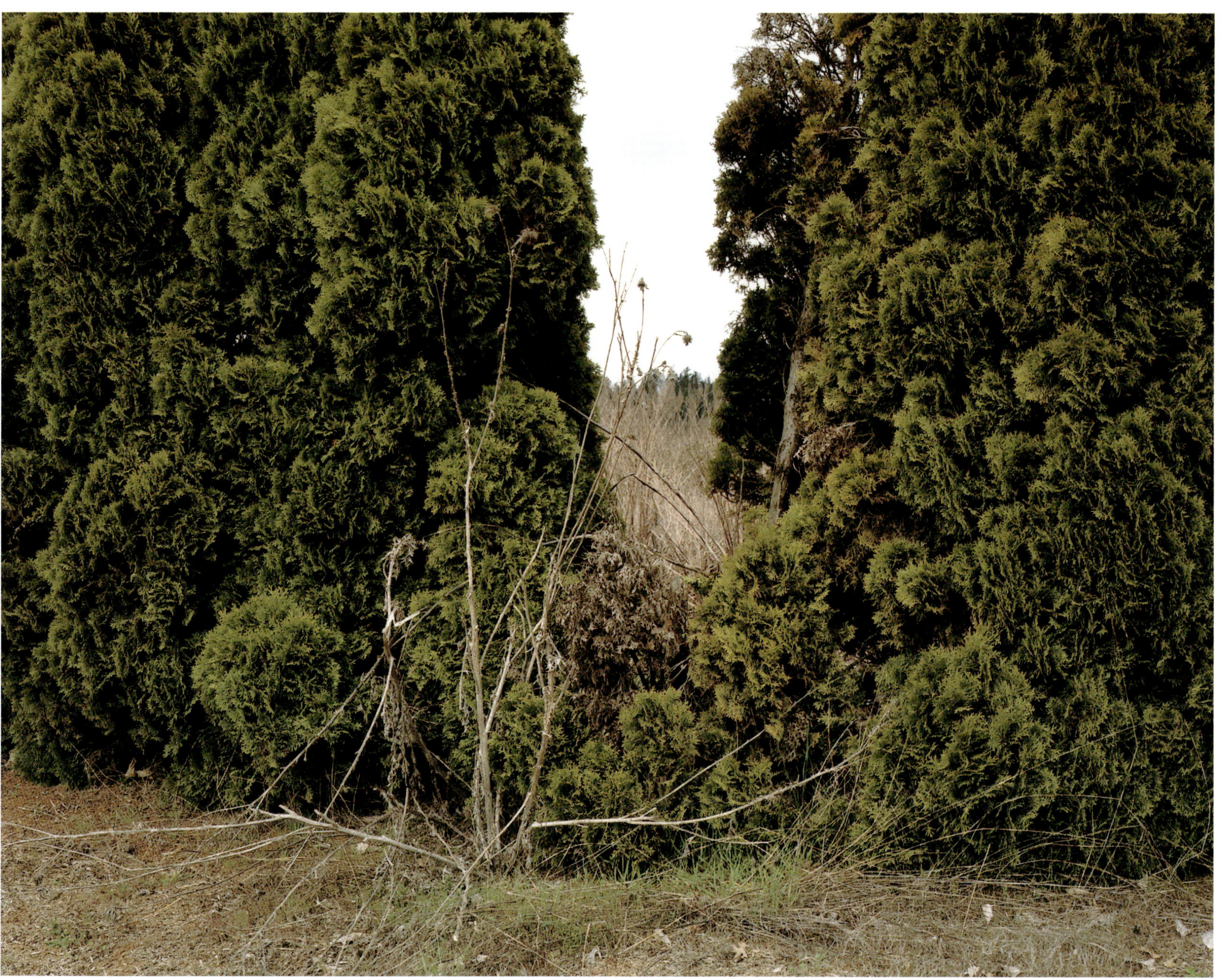

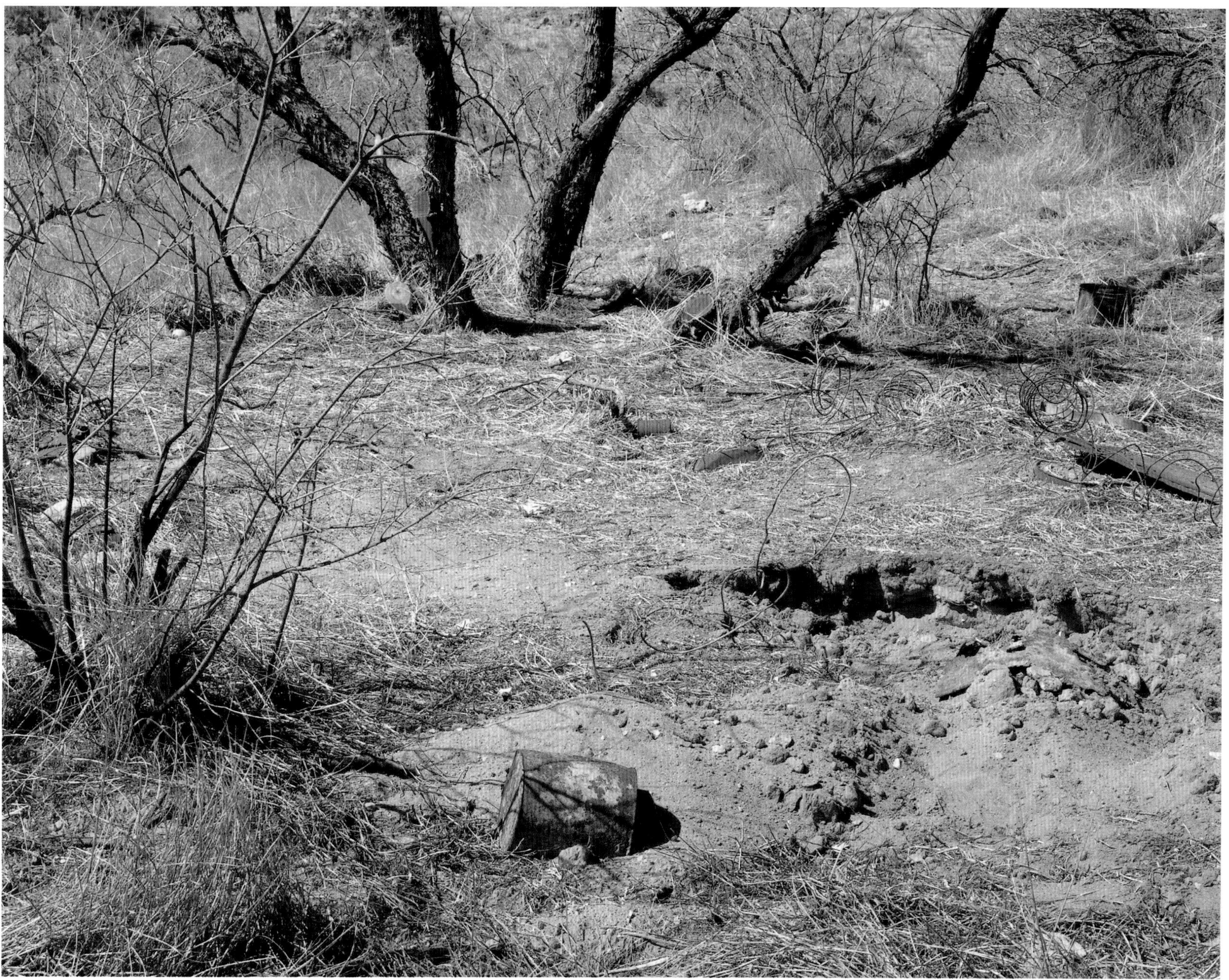

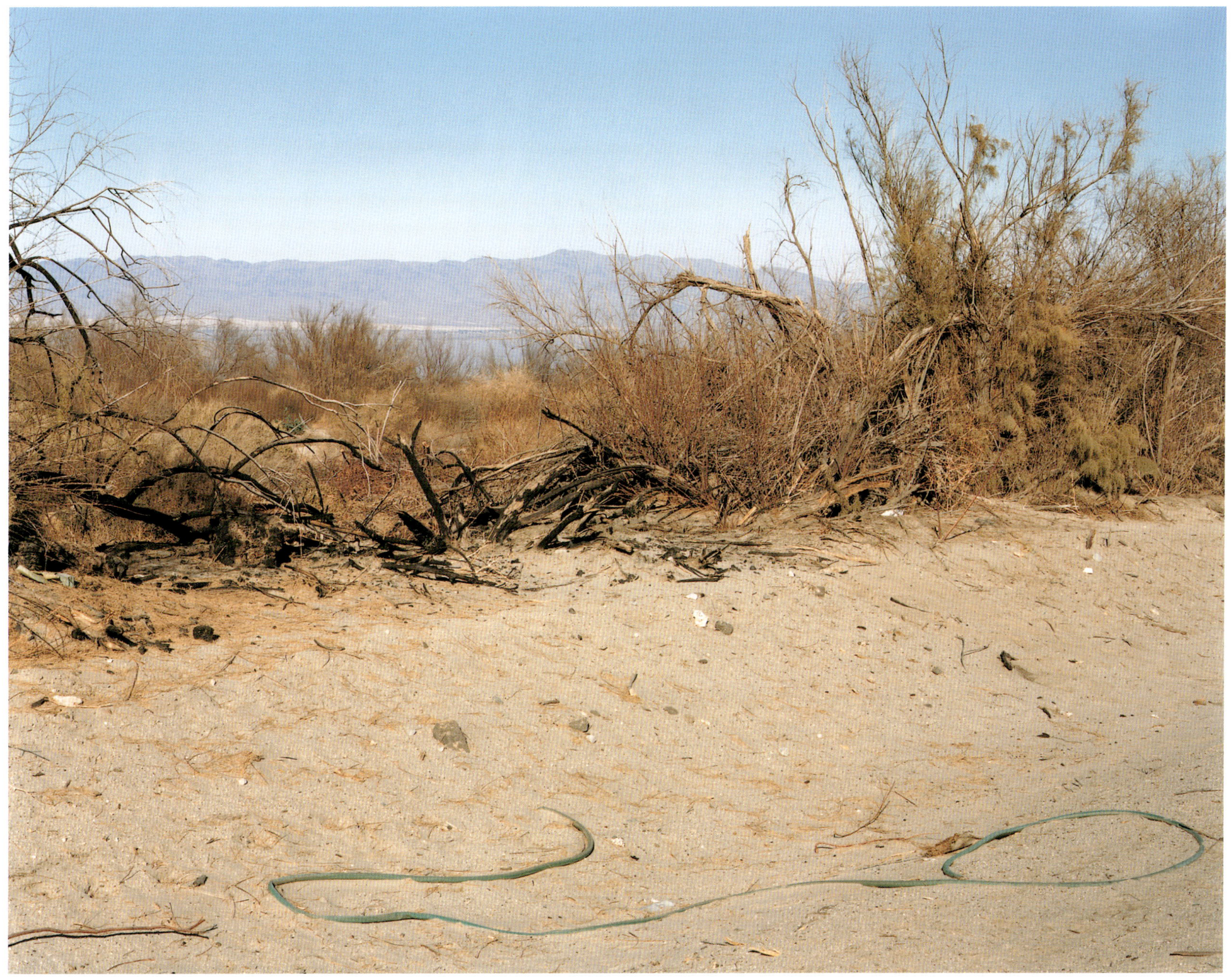

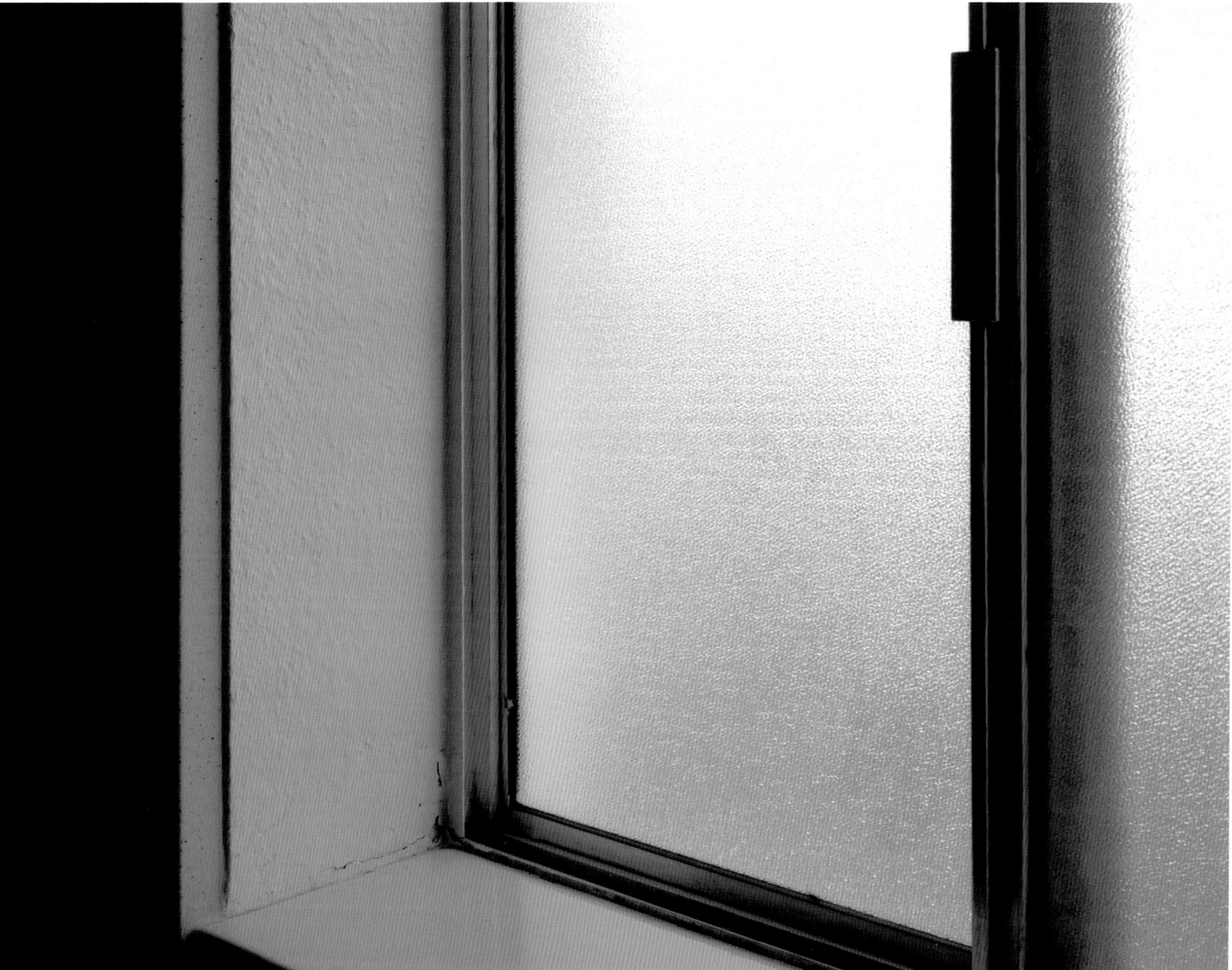

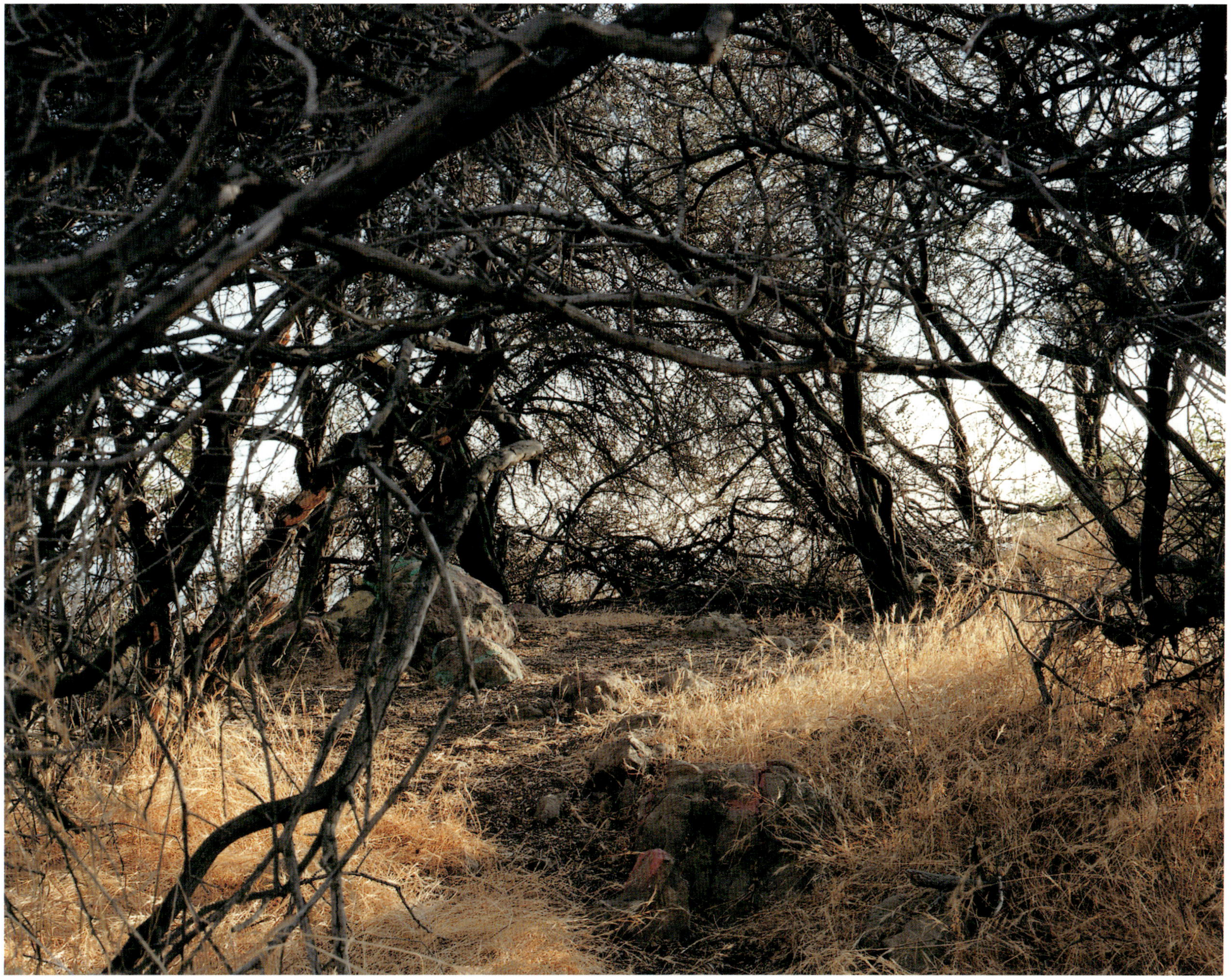

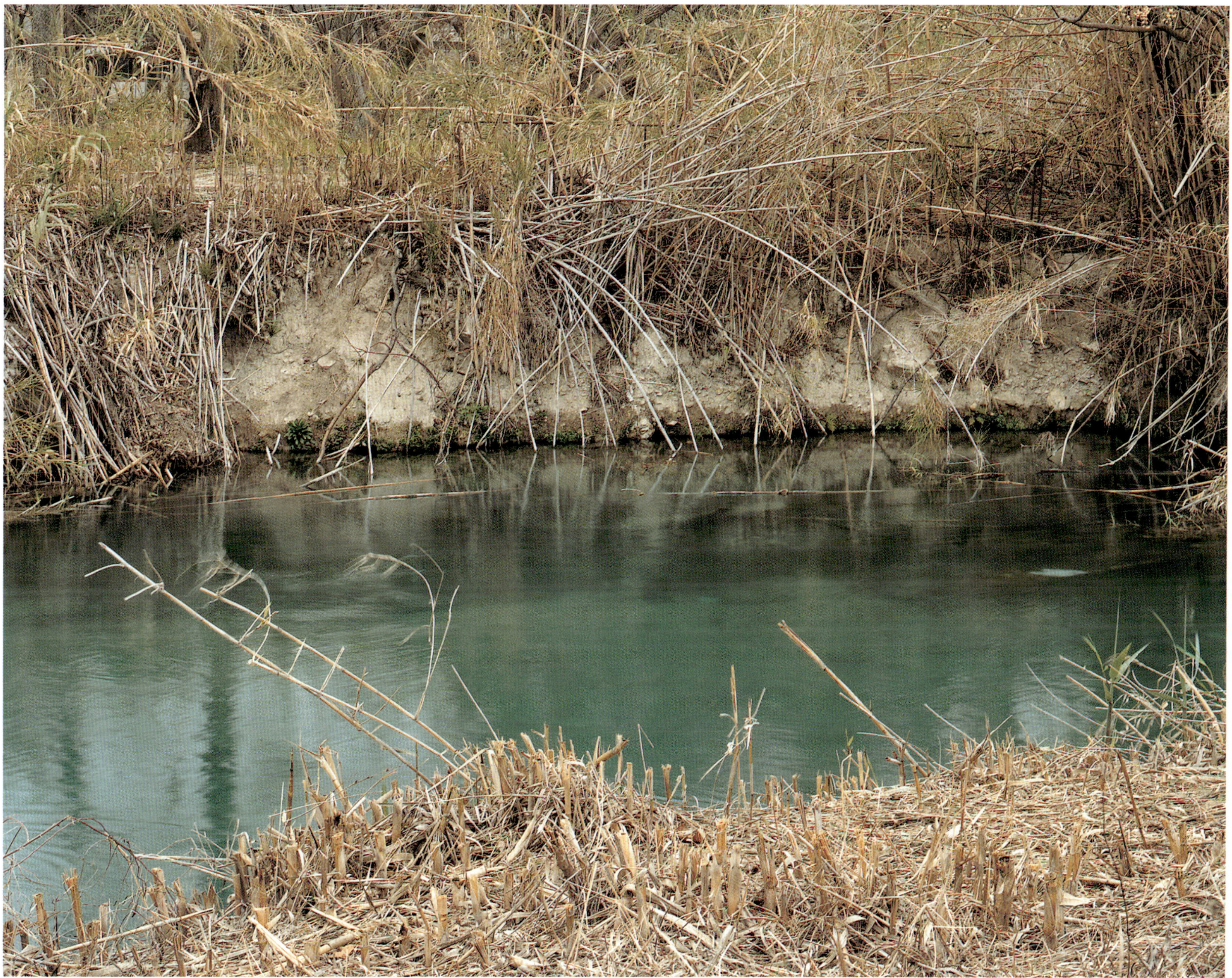

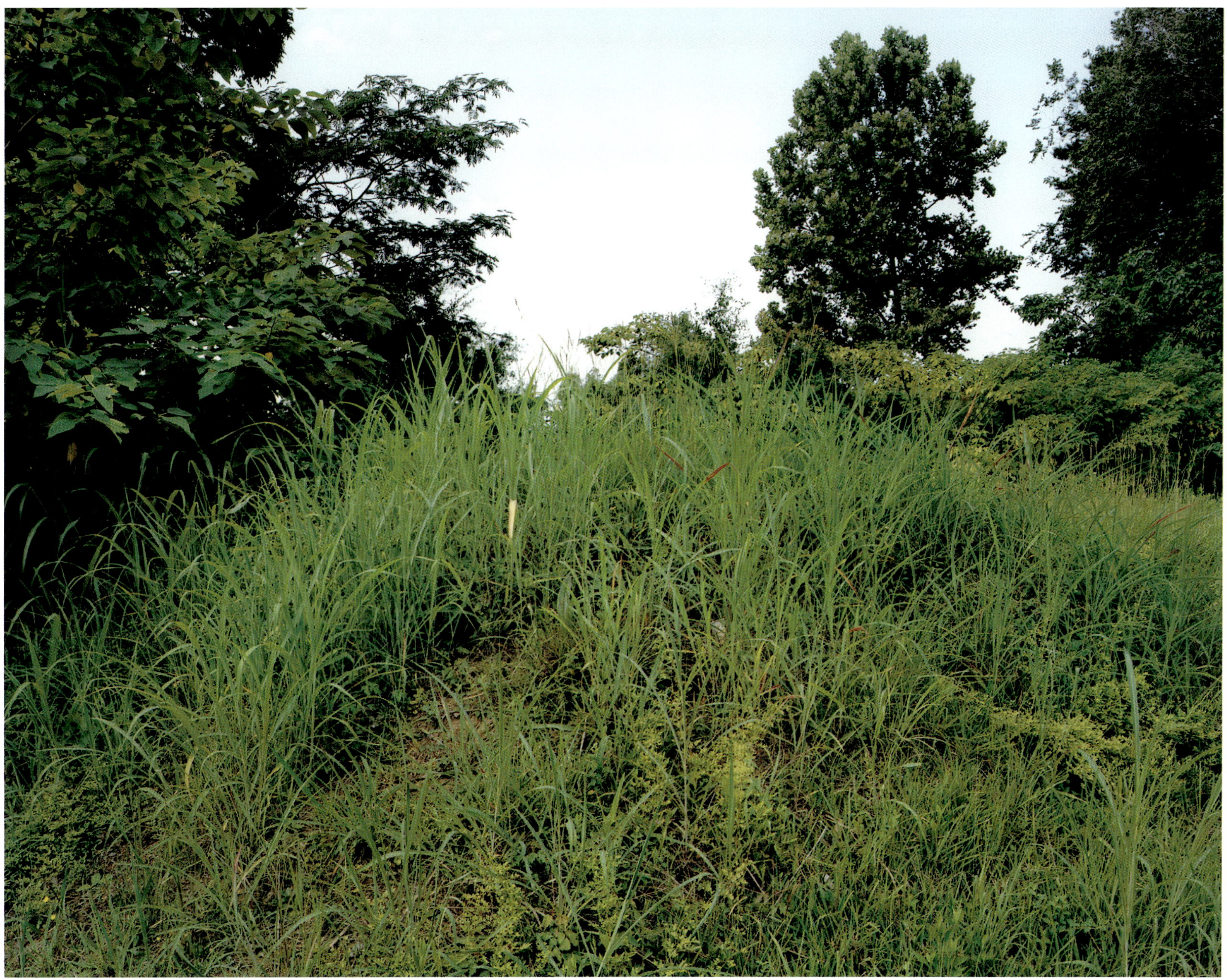

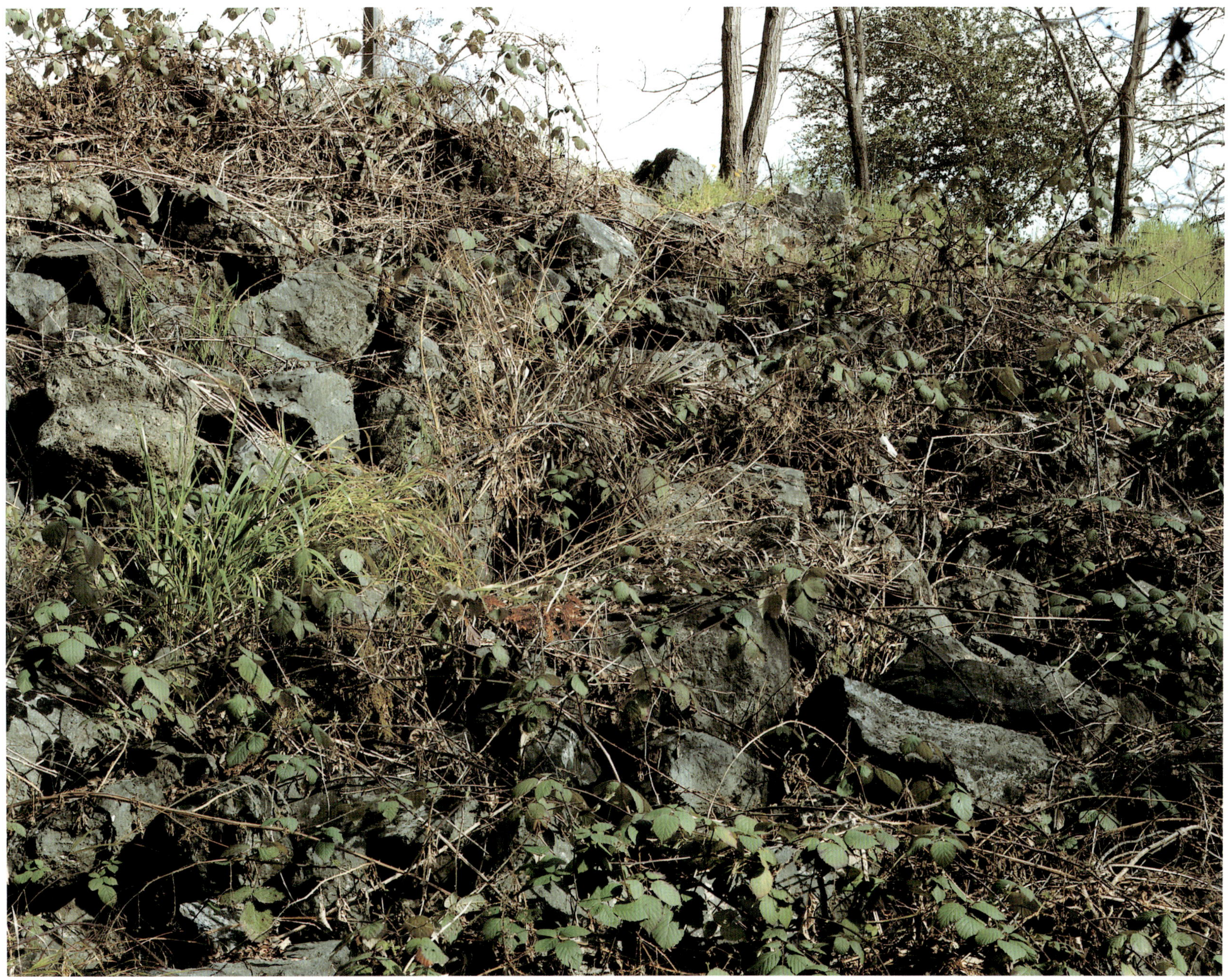

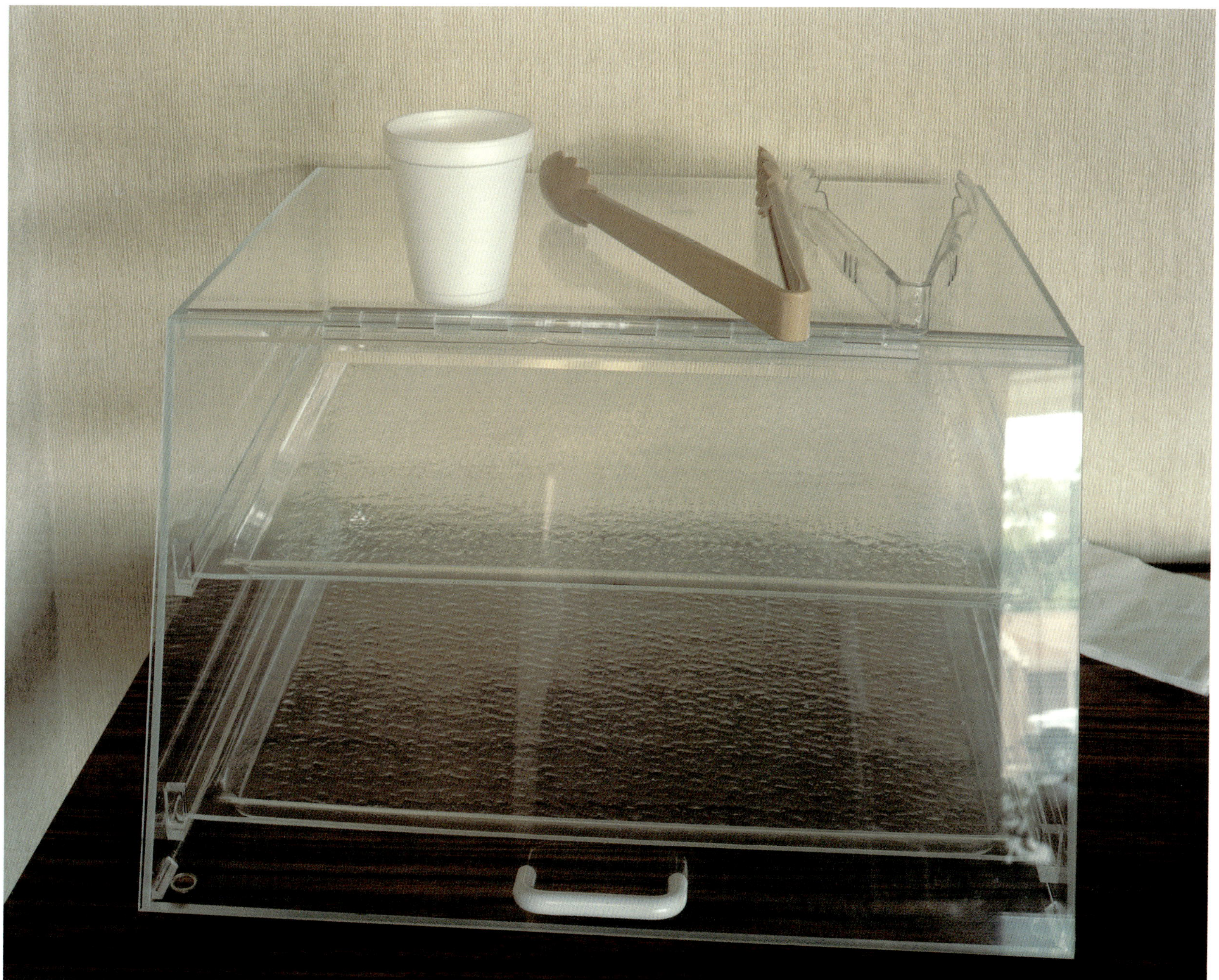

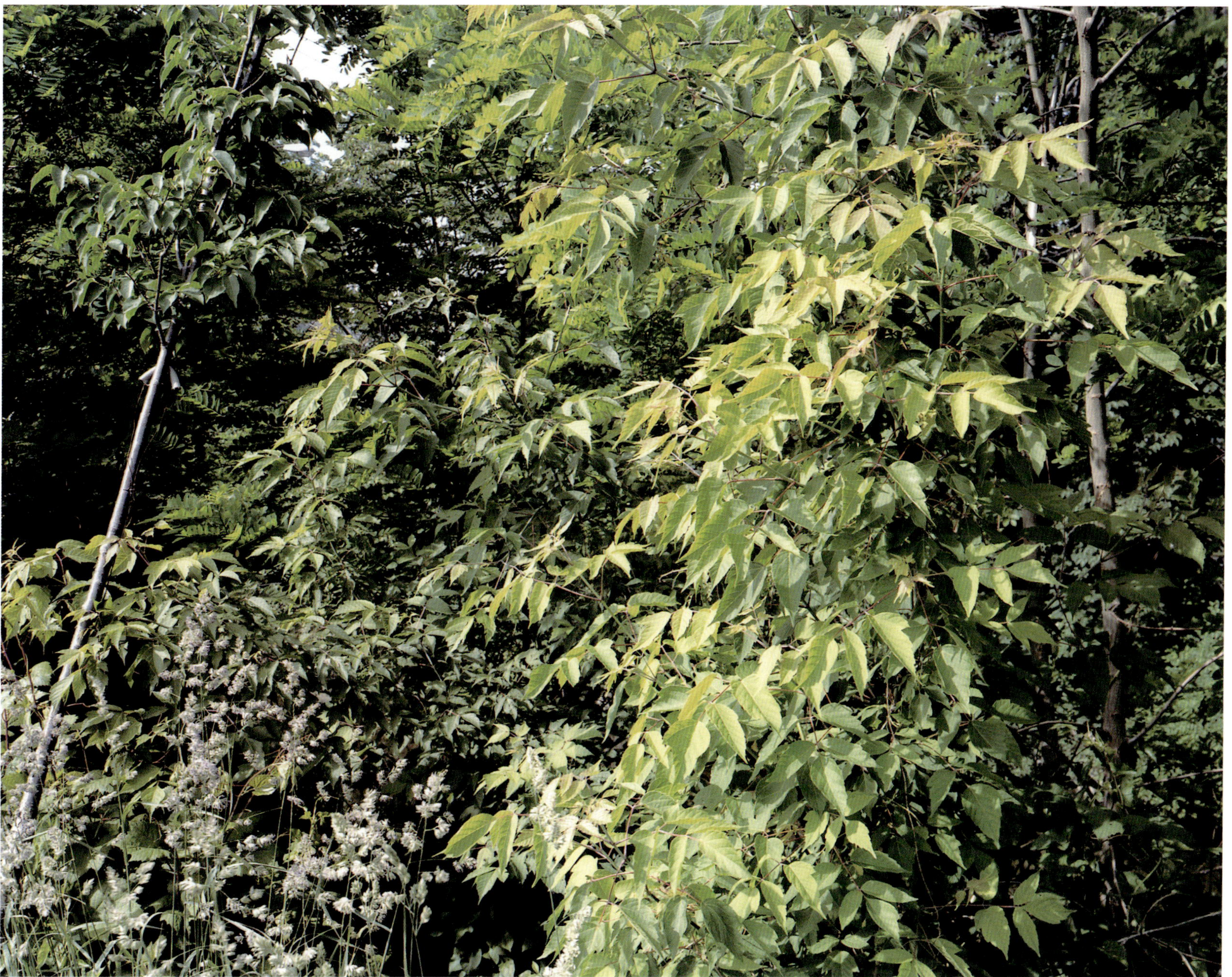

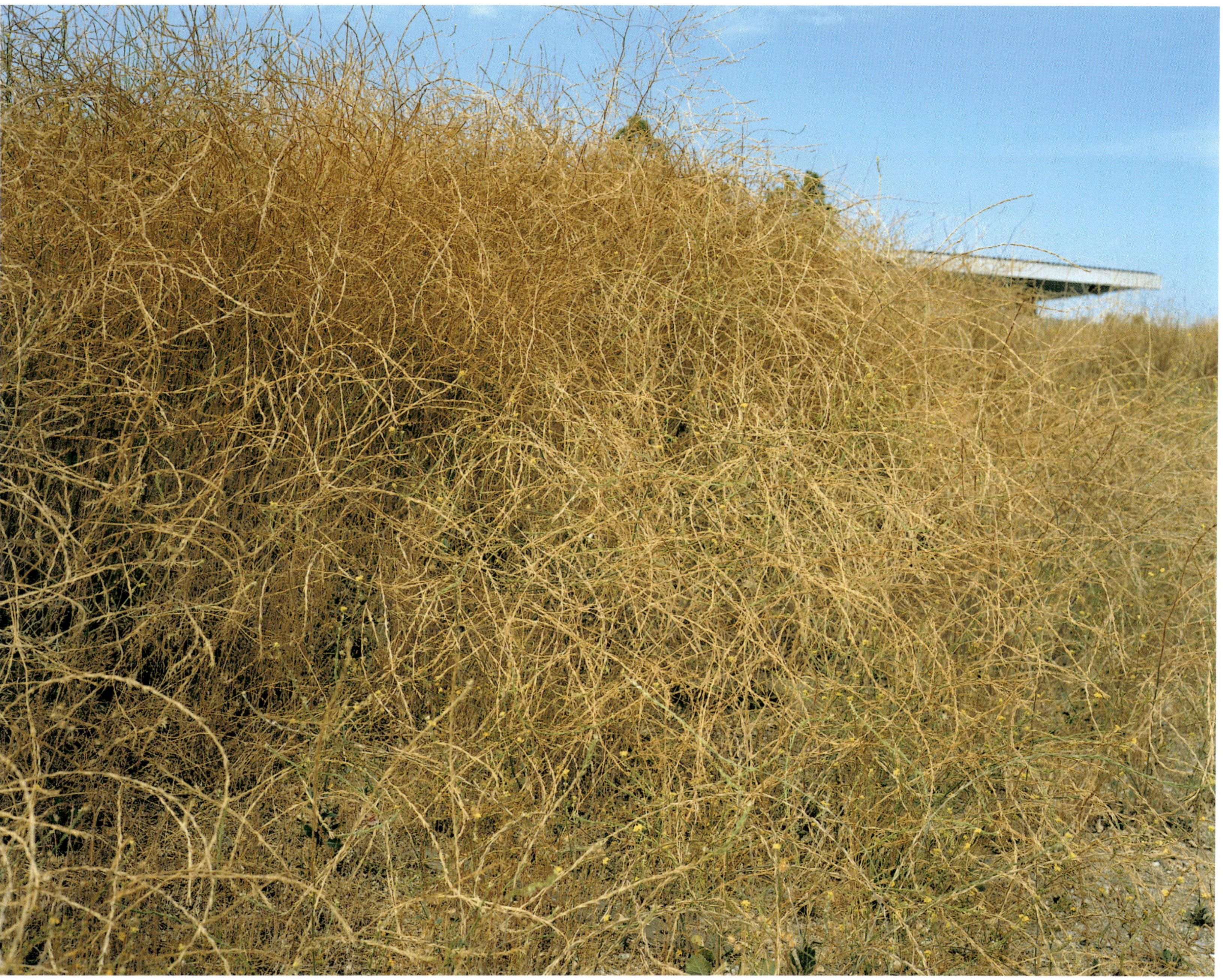

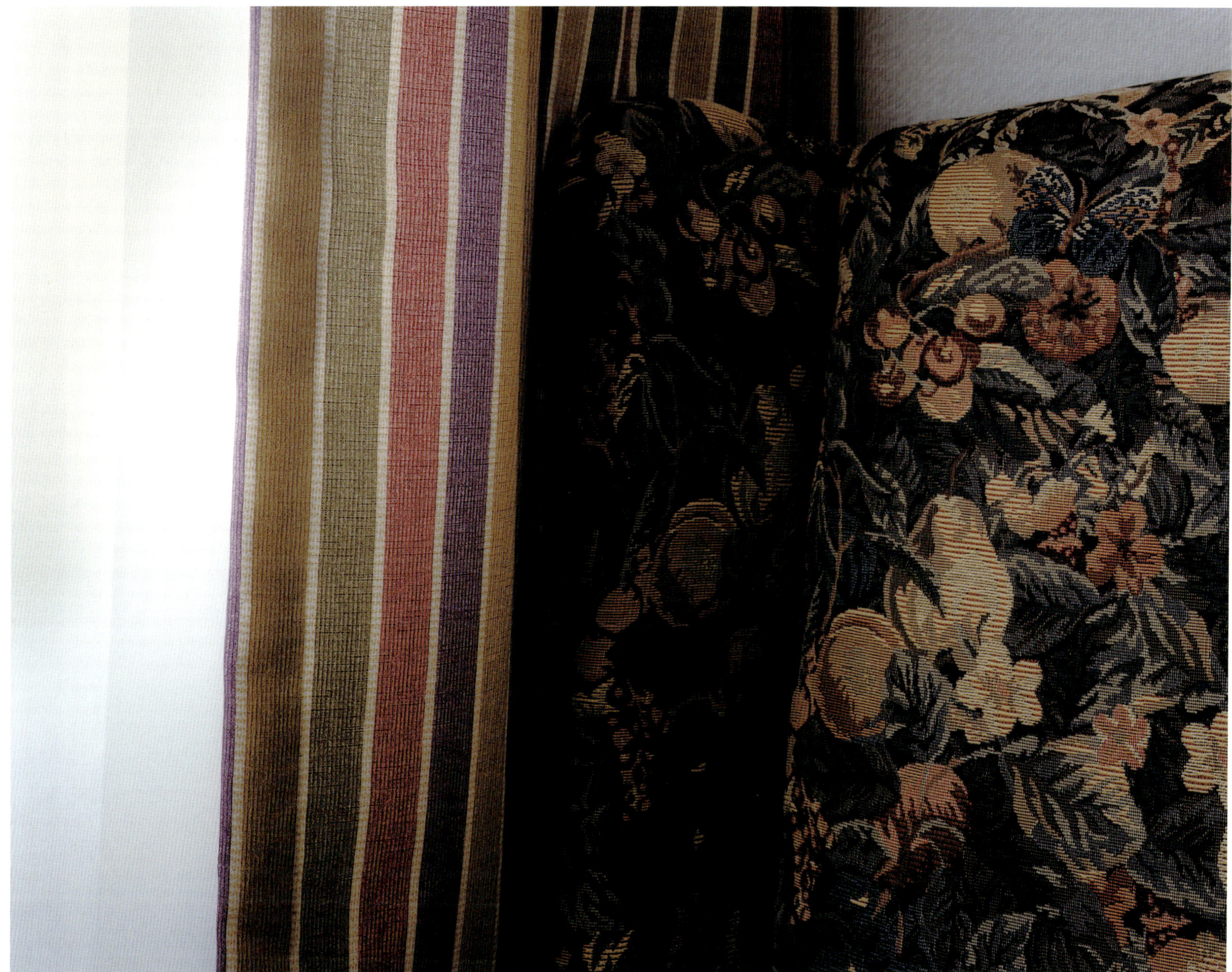

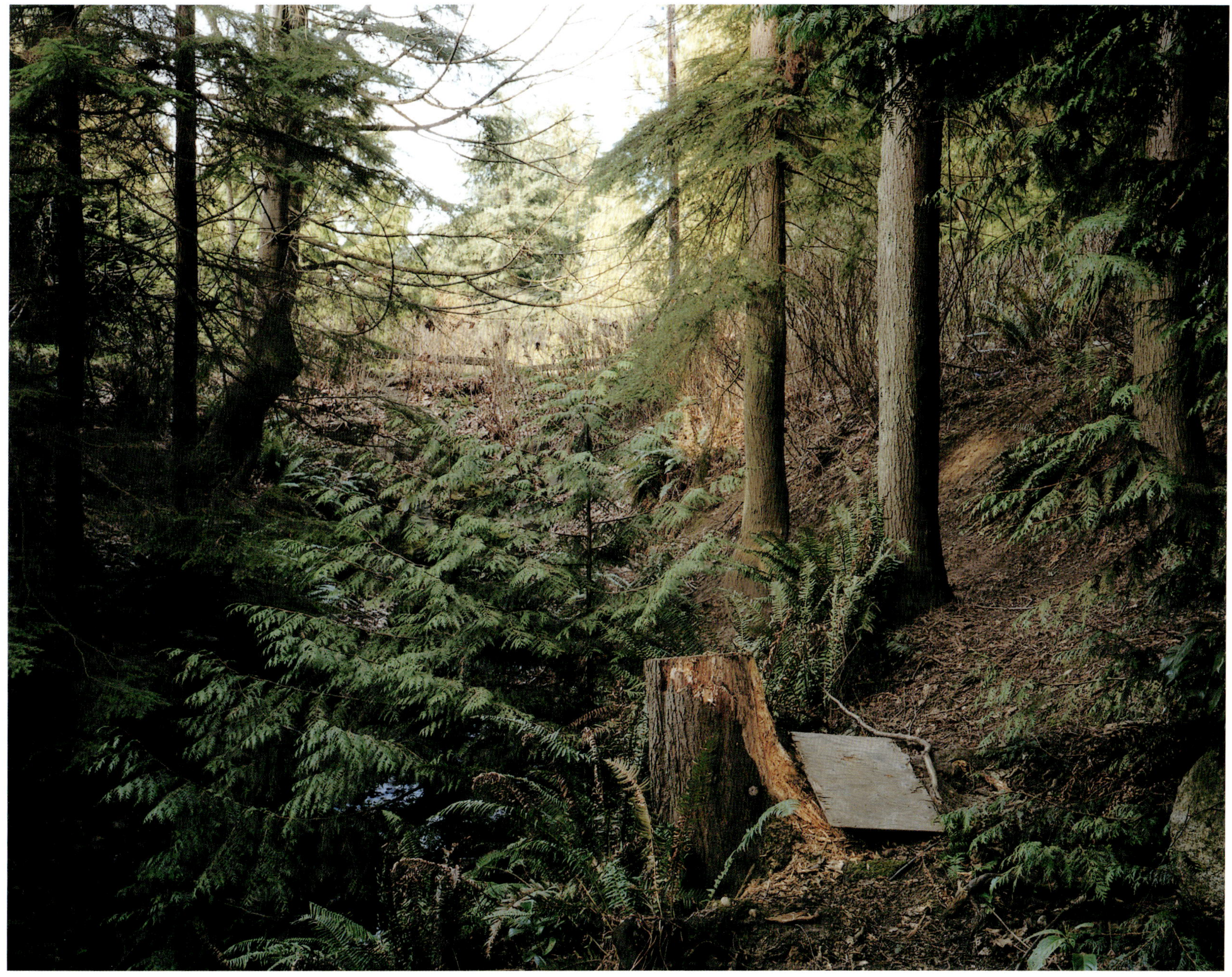

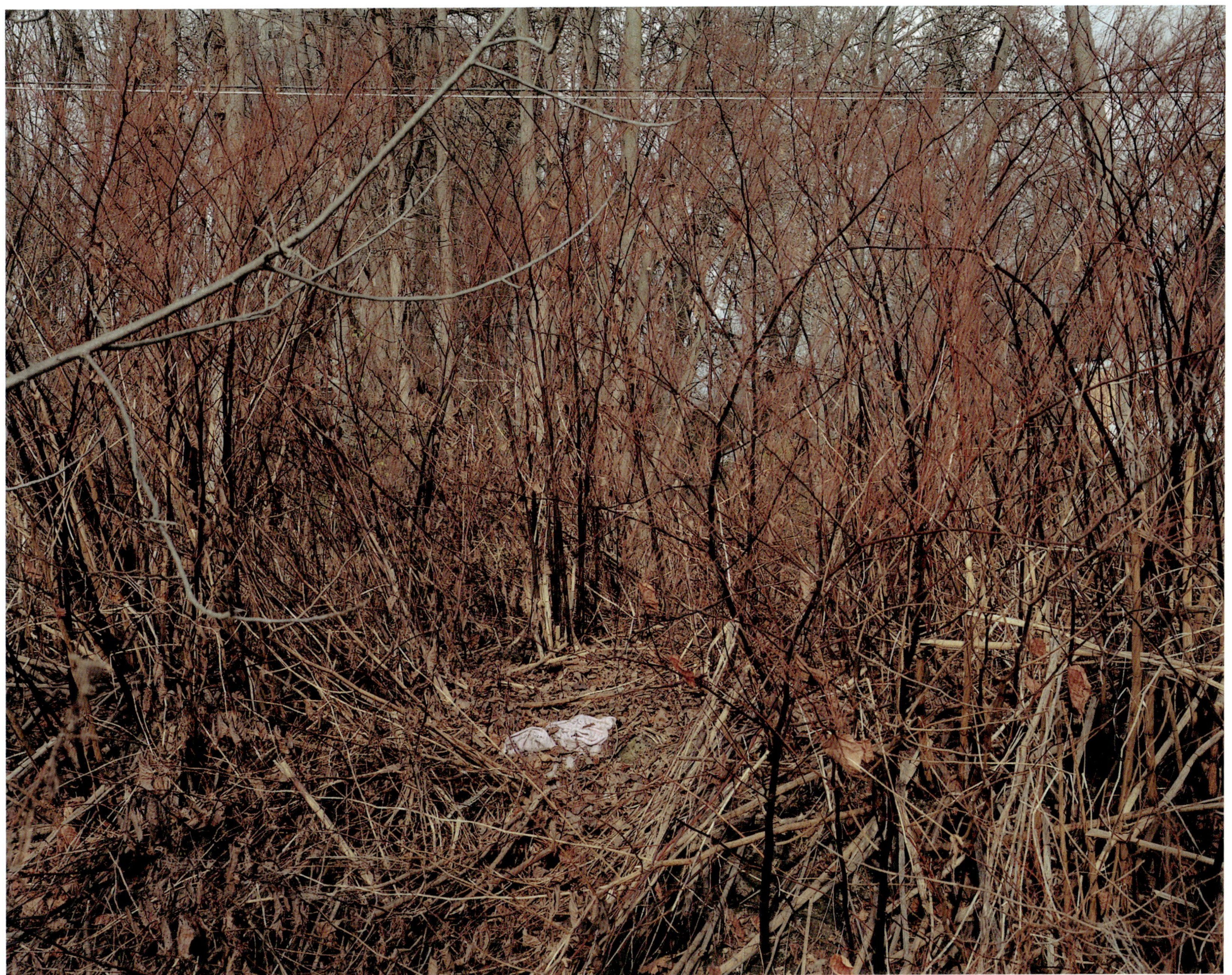

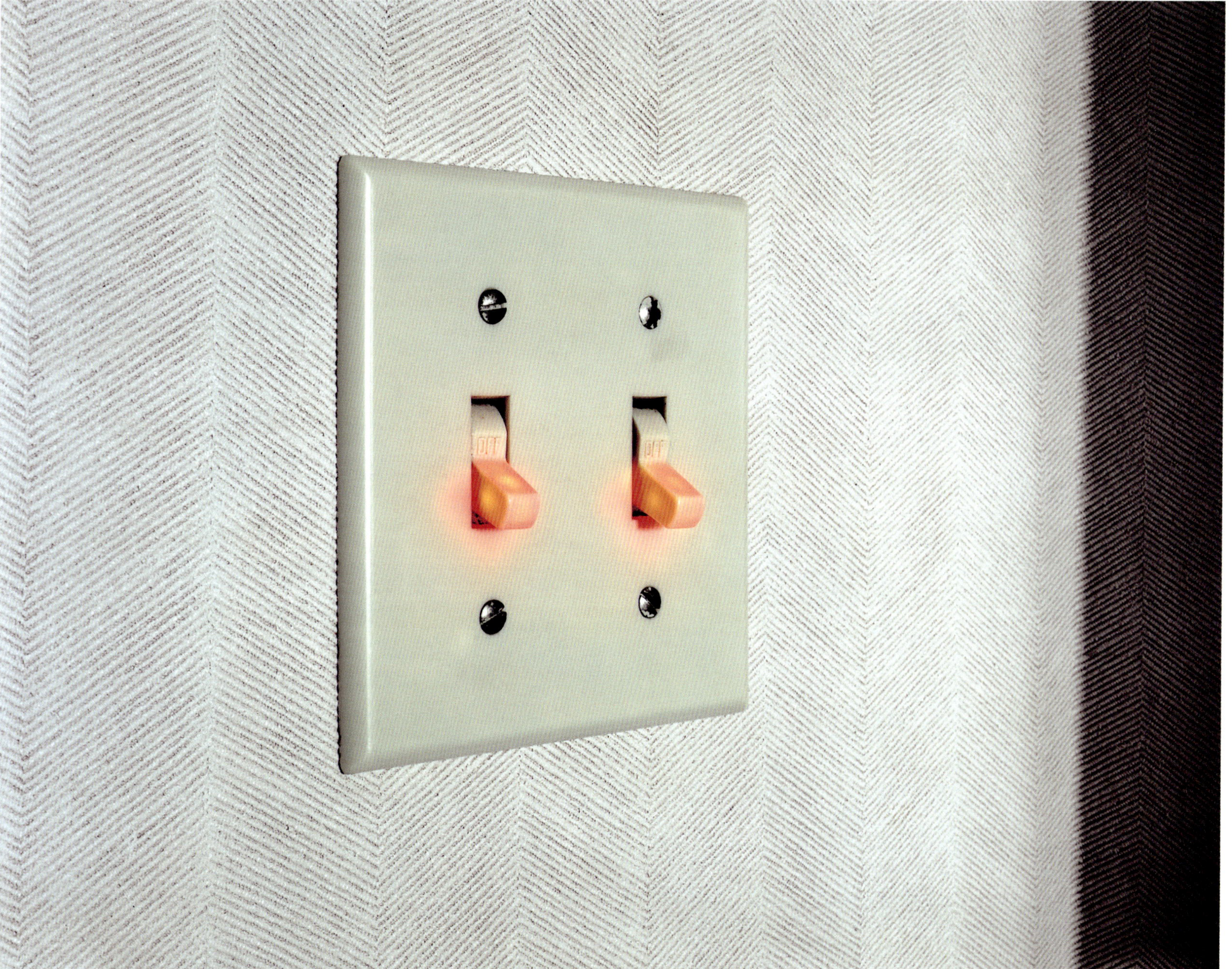

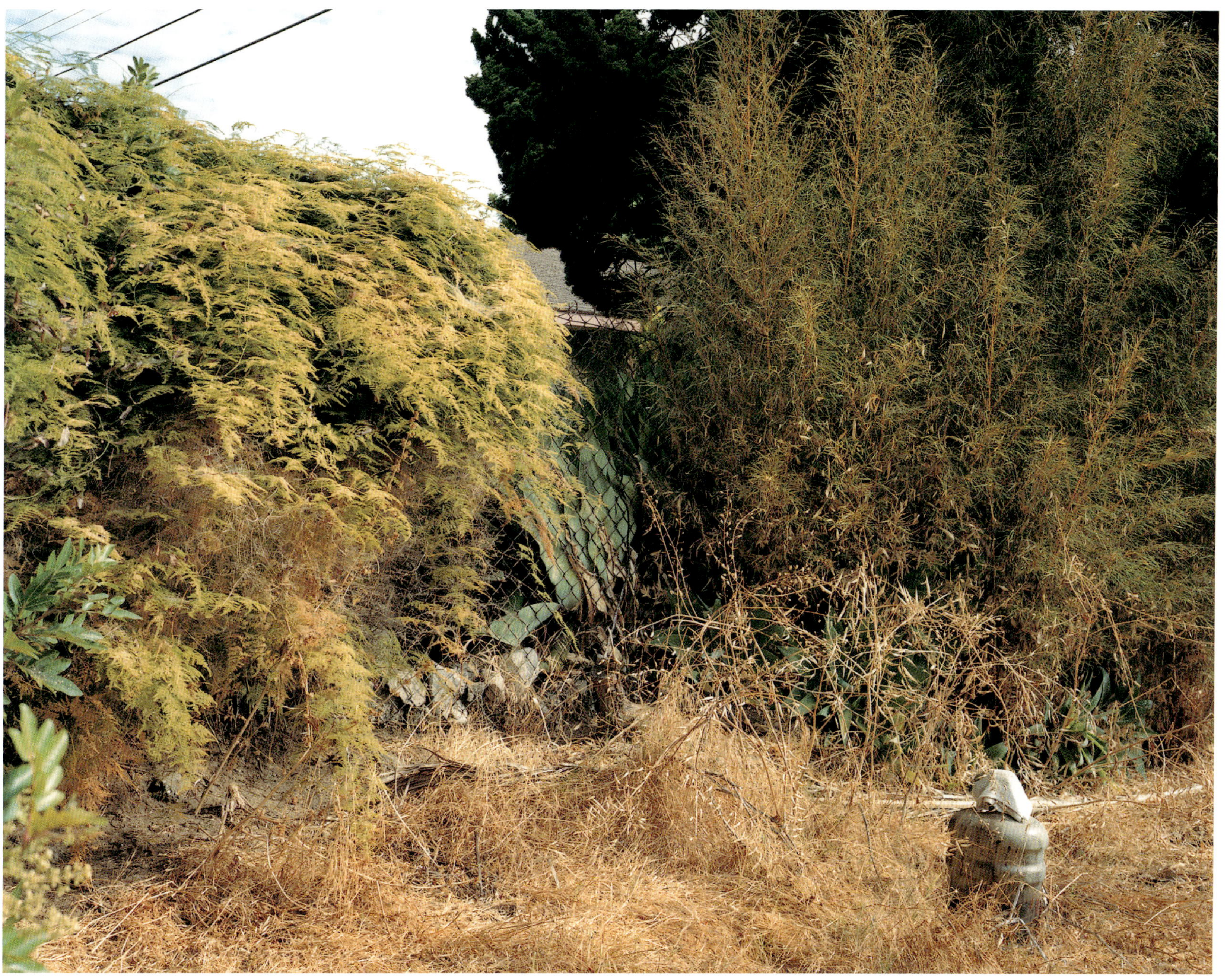

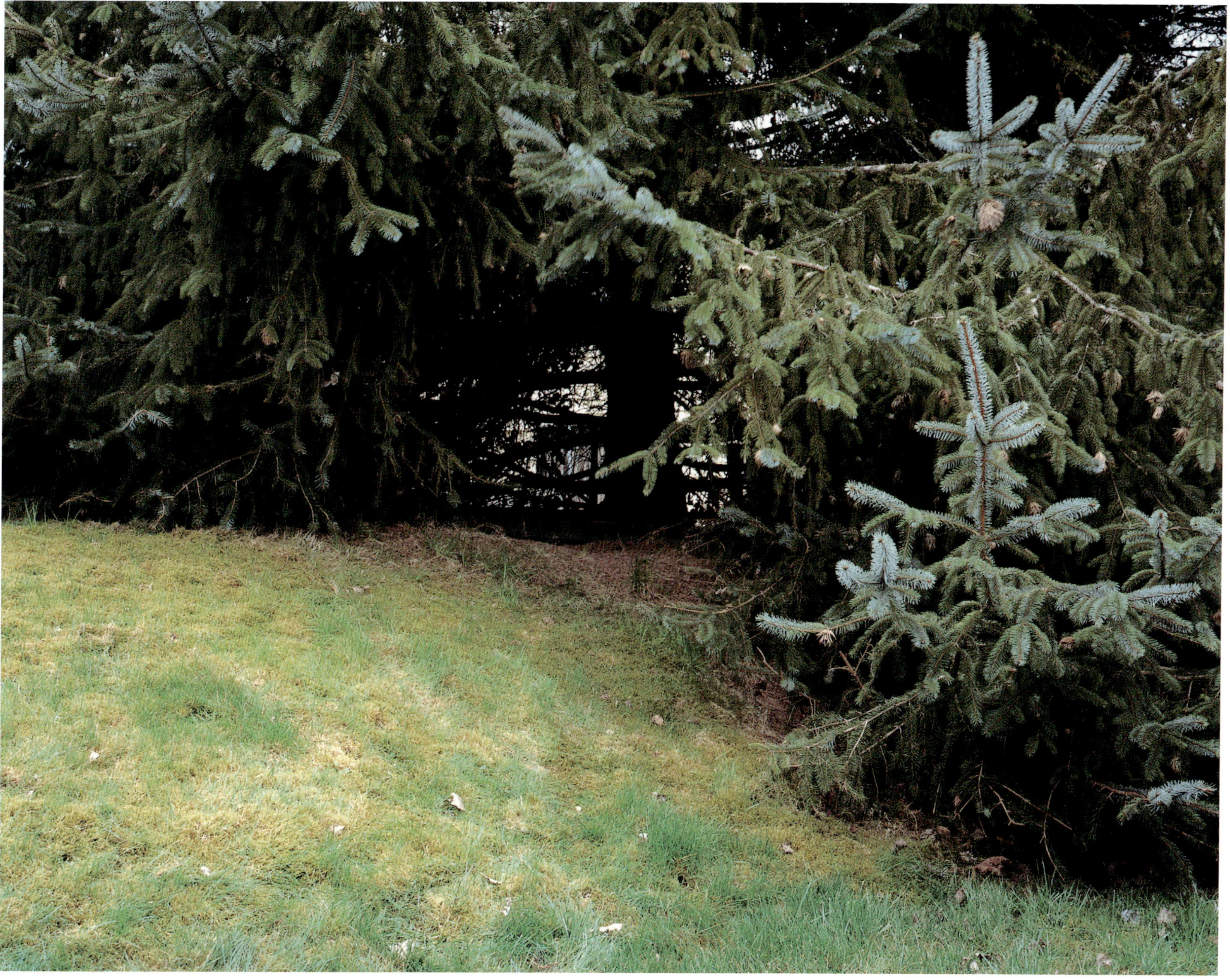

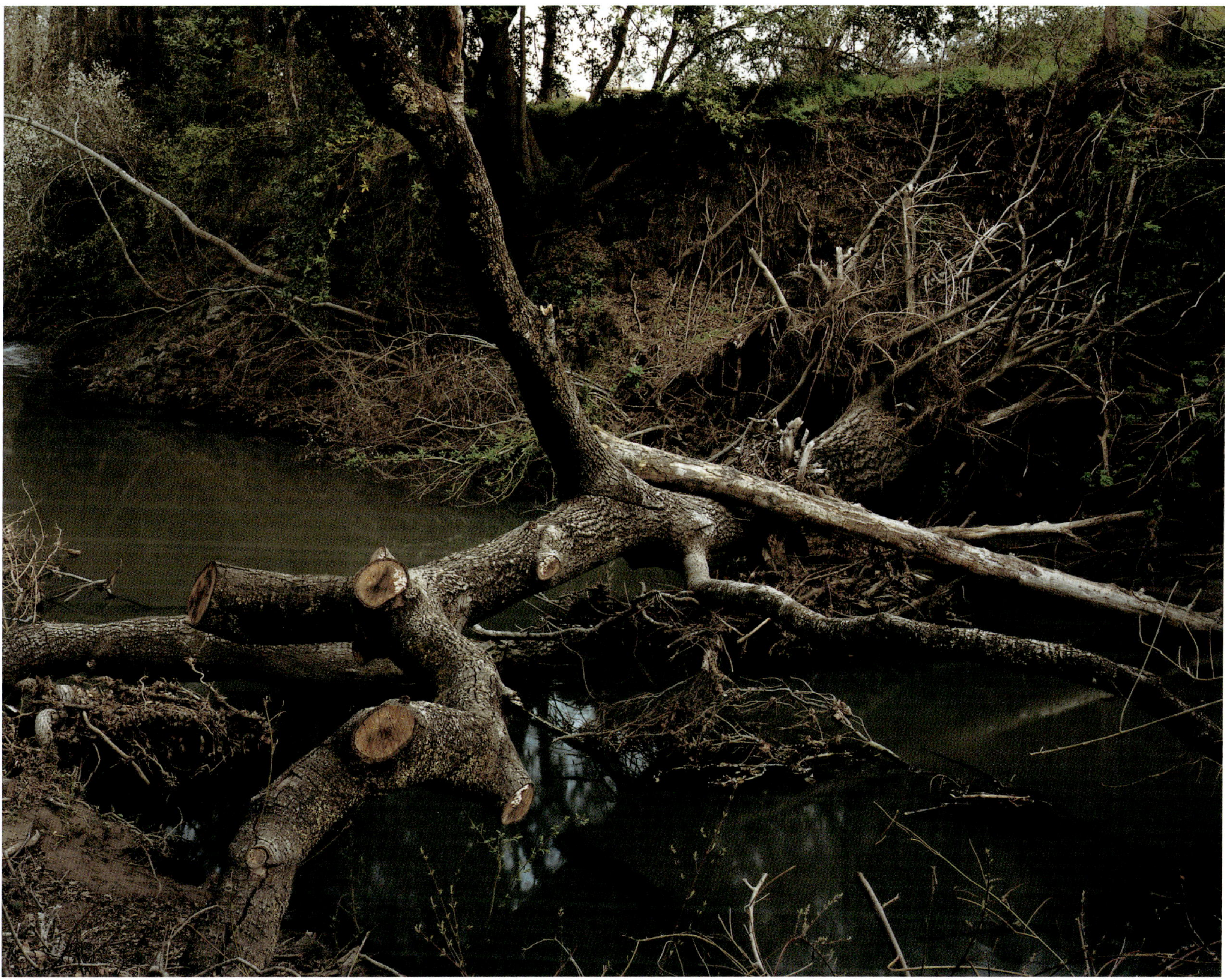

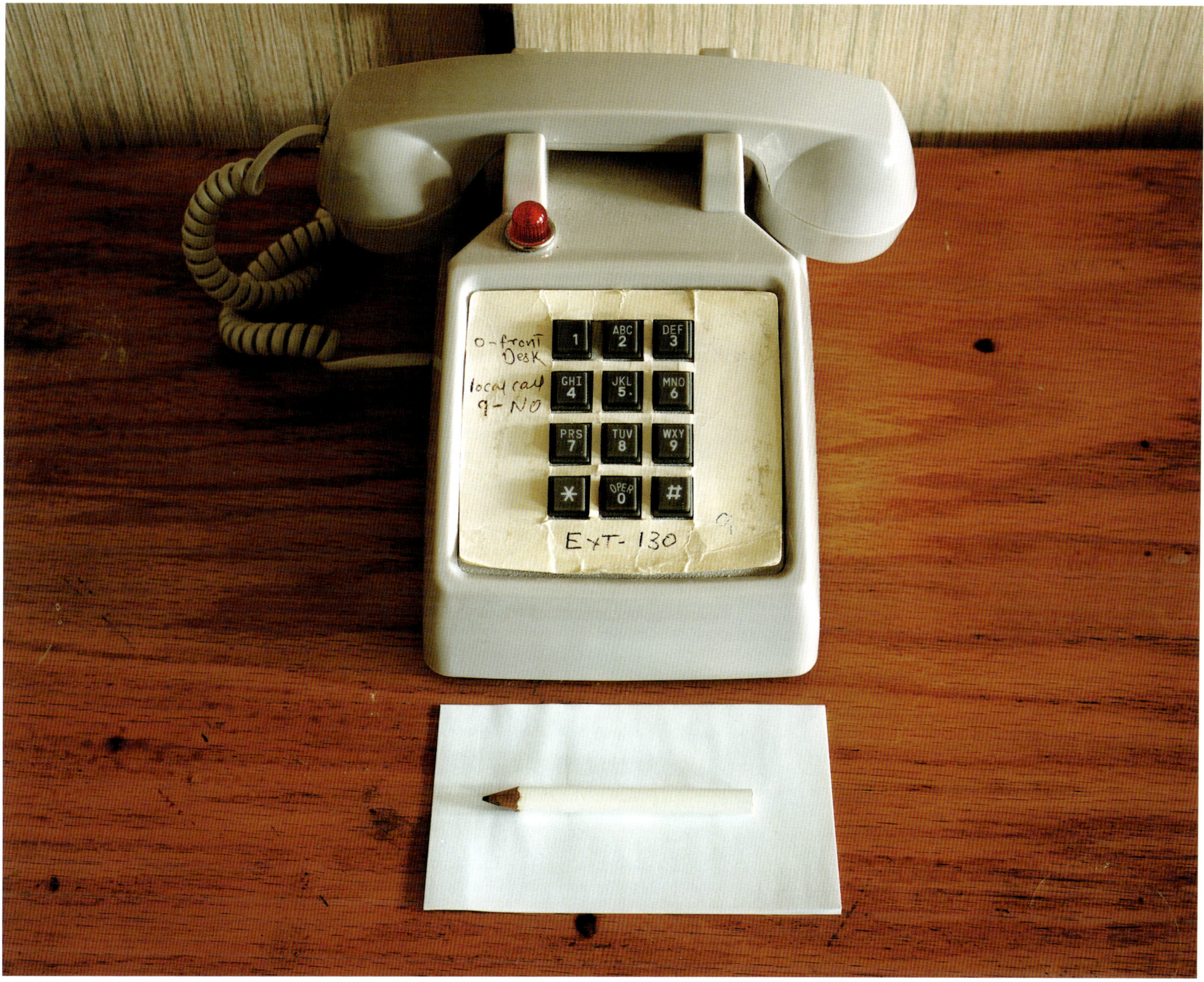
0-front Desk
local call 9-NO
1
ABC 2
DEF 3
GHI 4
JKL 5
MNO 6
PRS 7
TUV 8
WXY 9
*
OPER 0
#
EXT-130

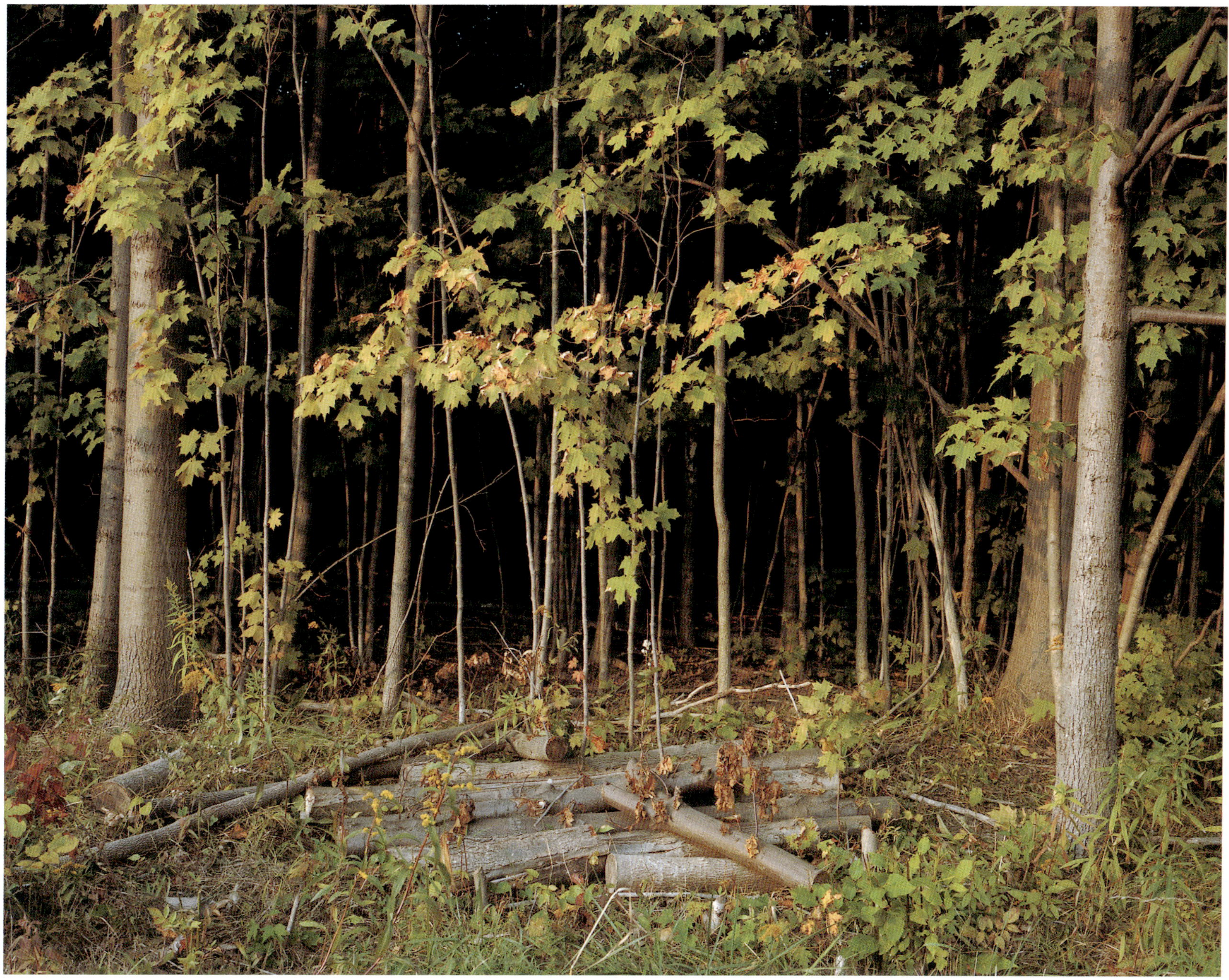

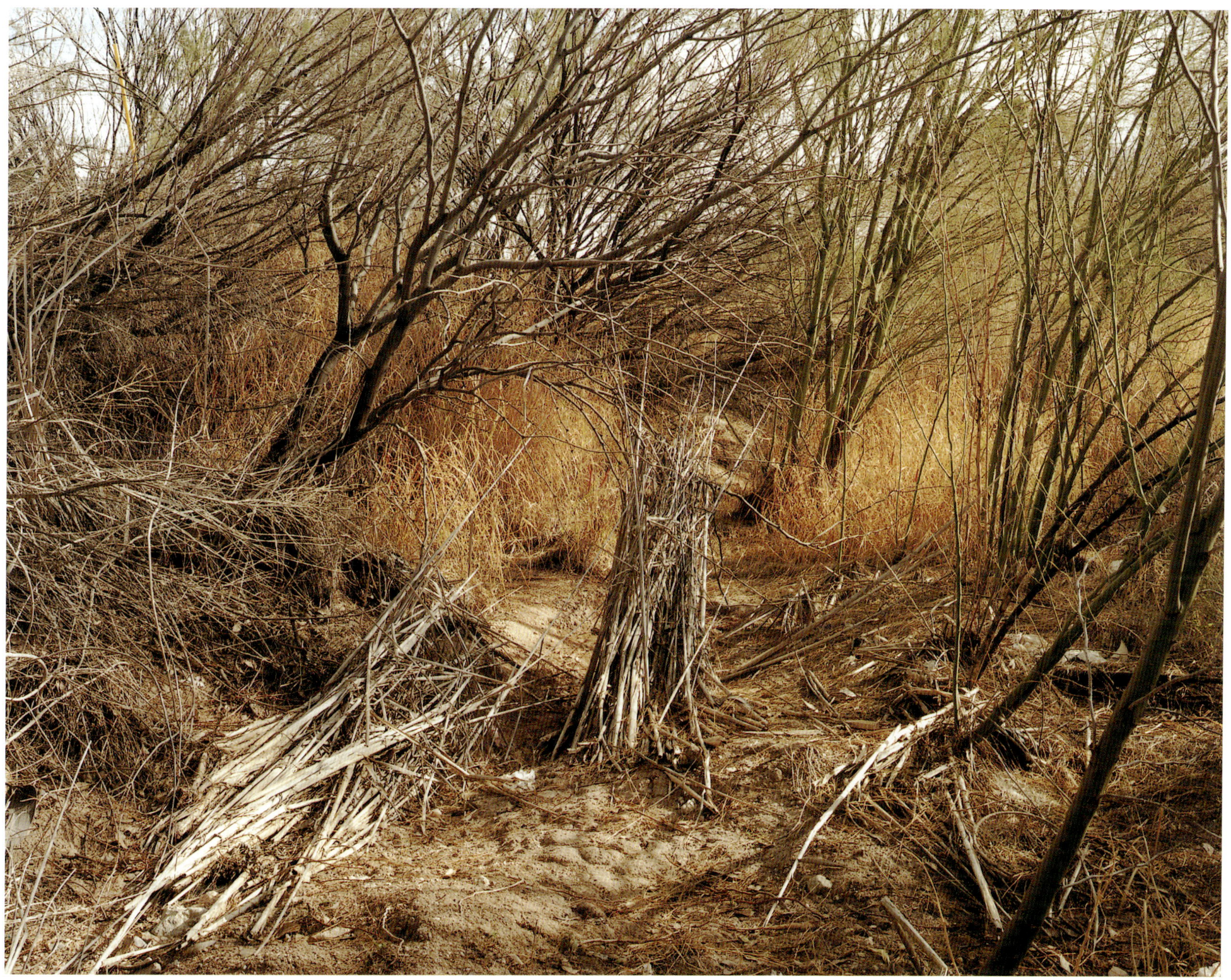

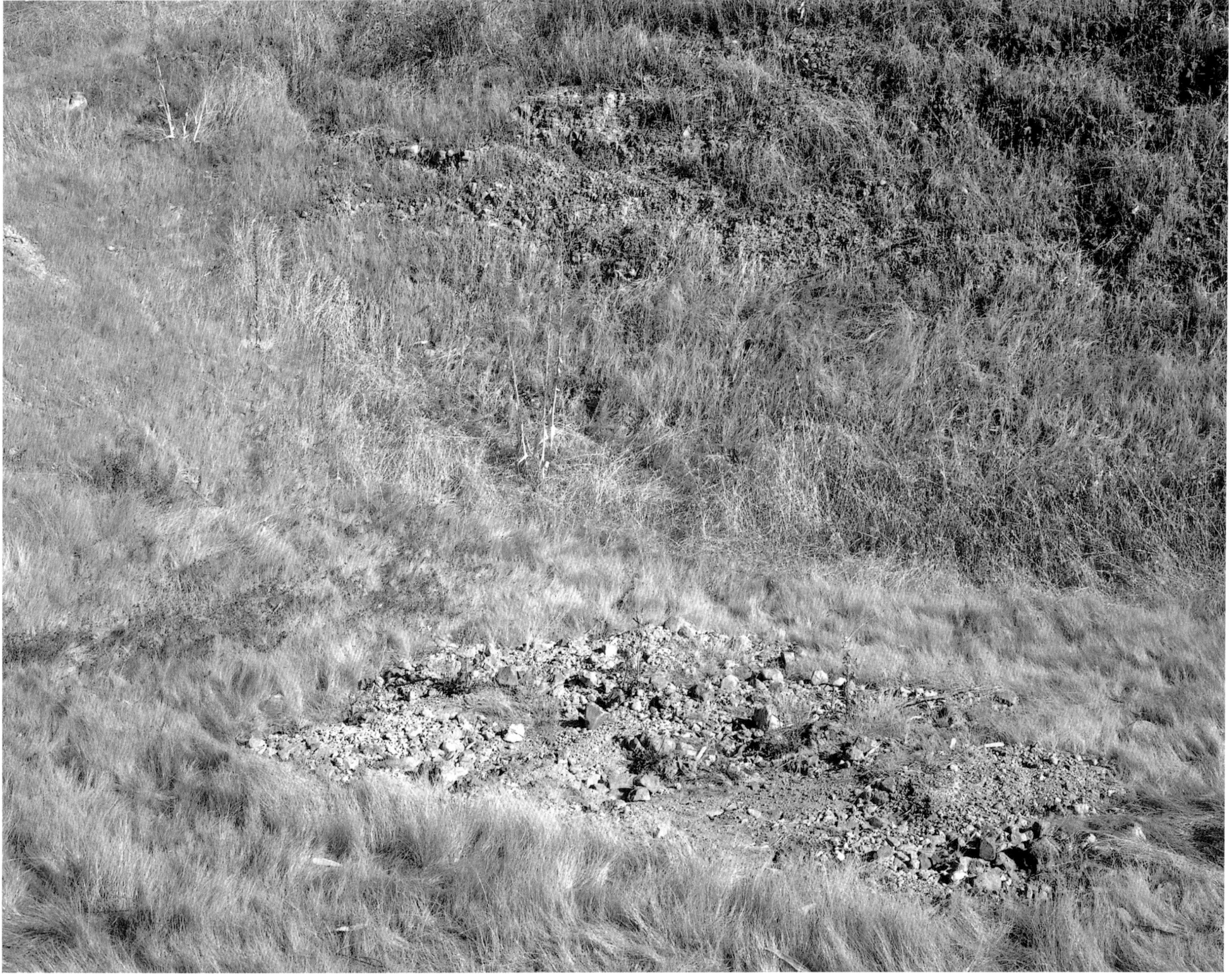

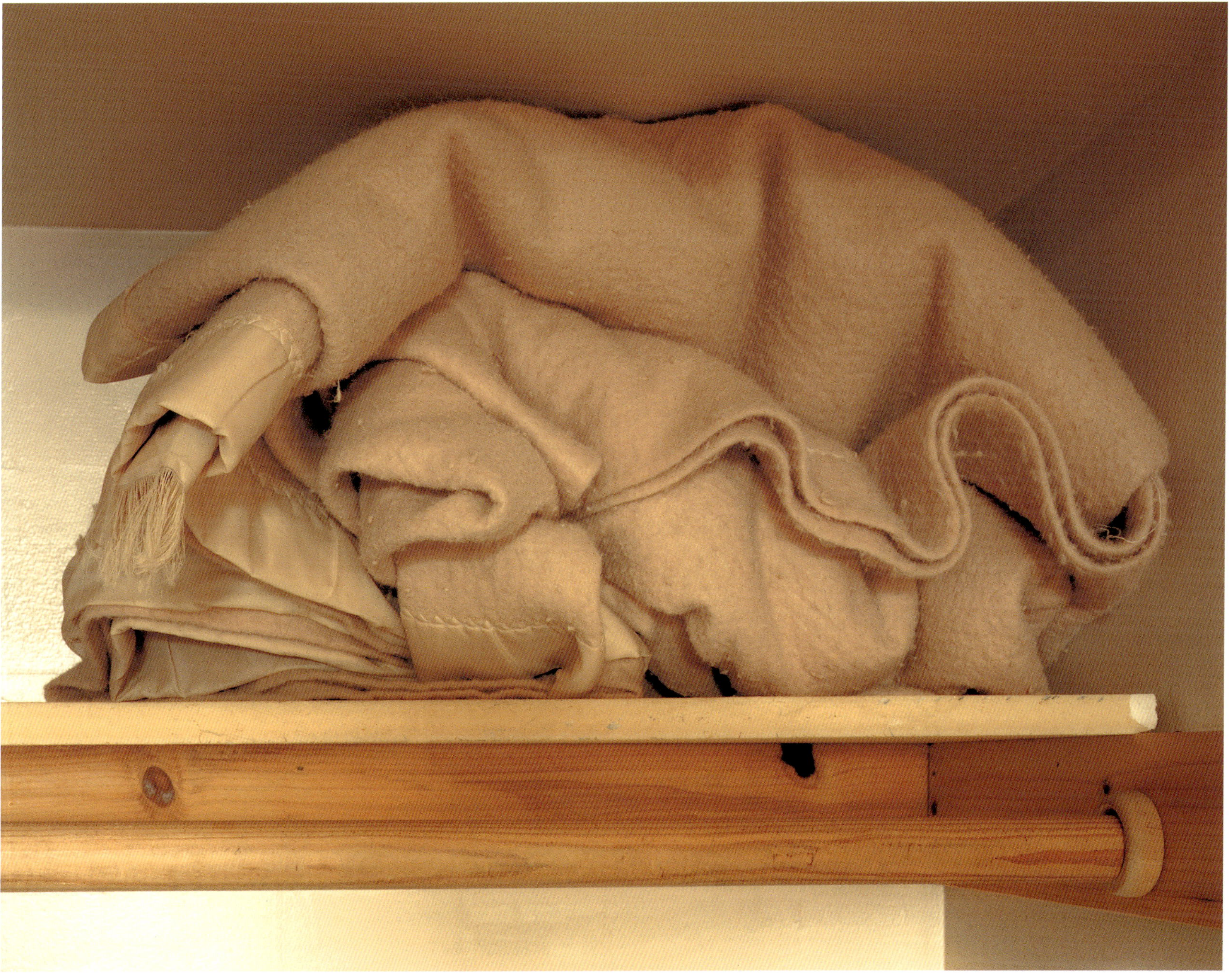

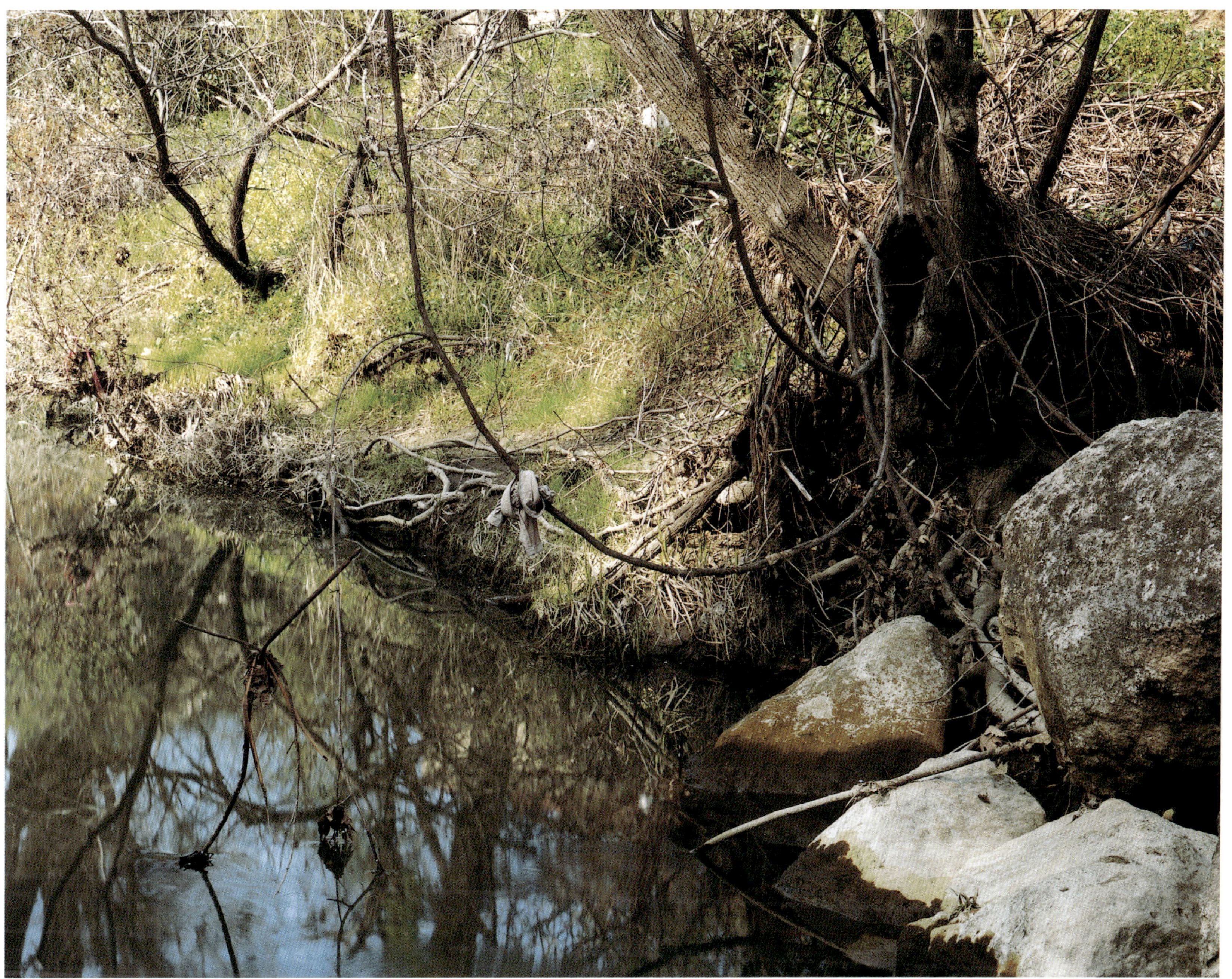

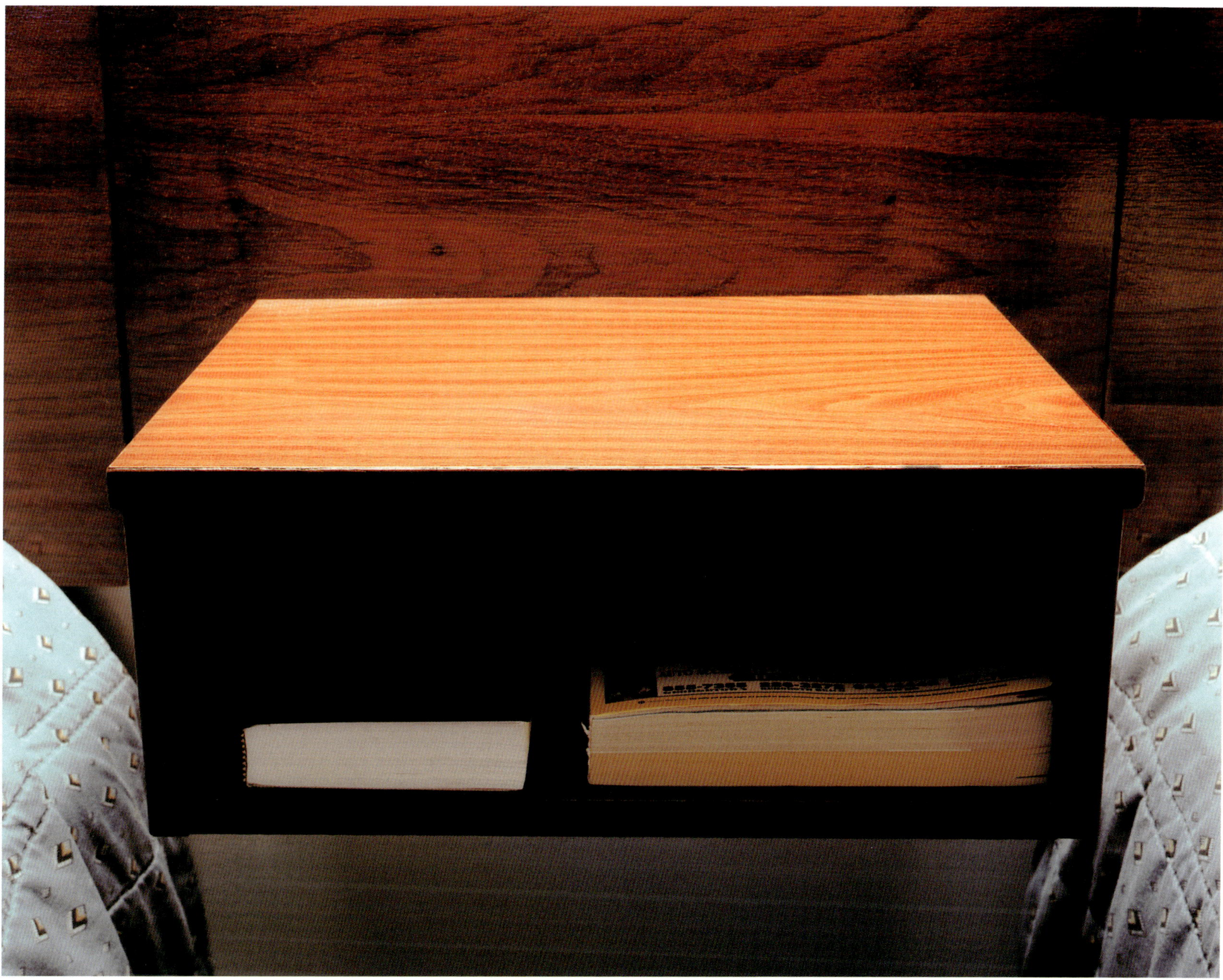

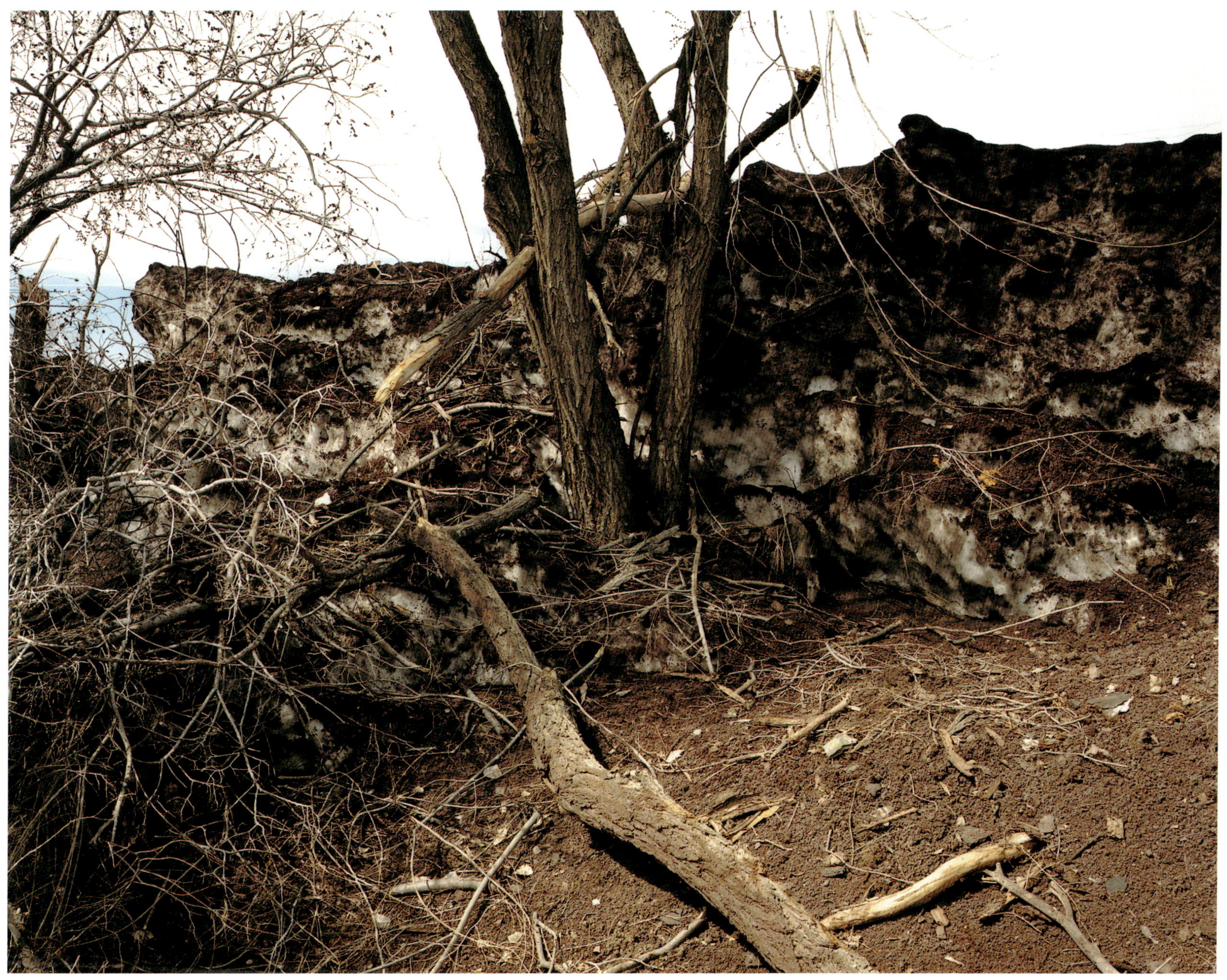

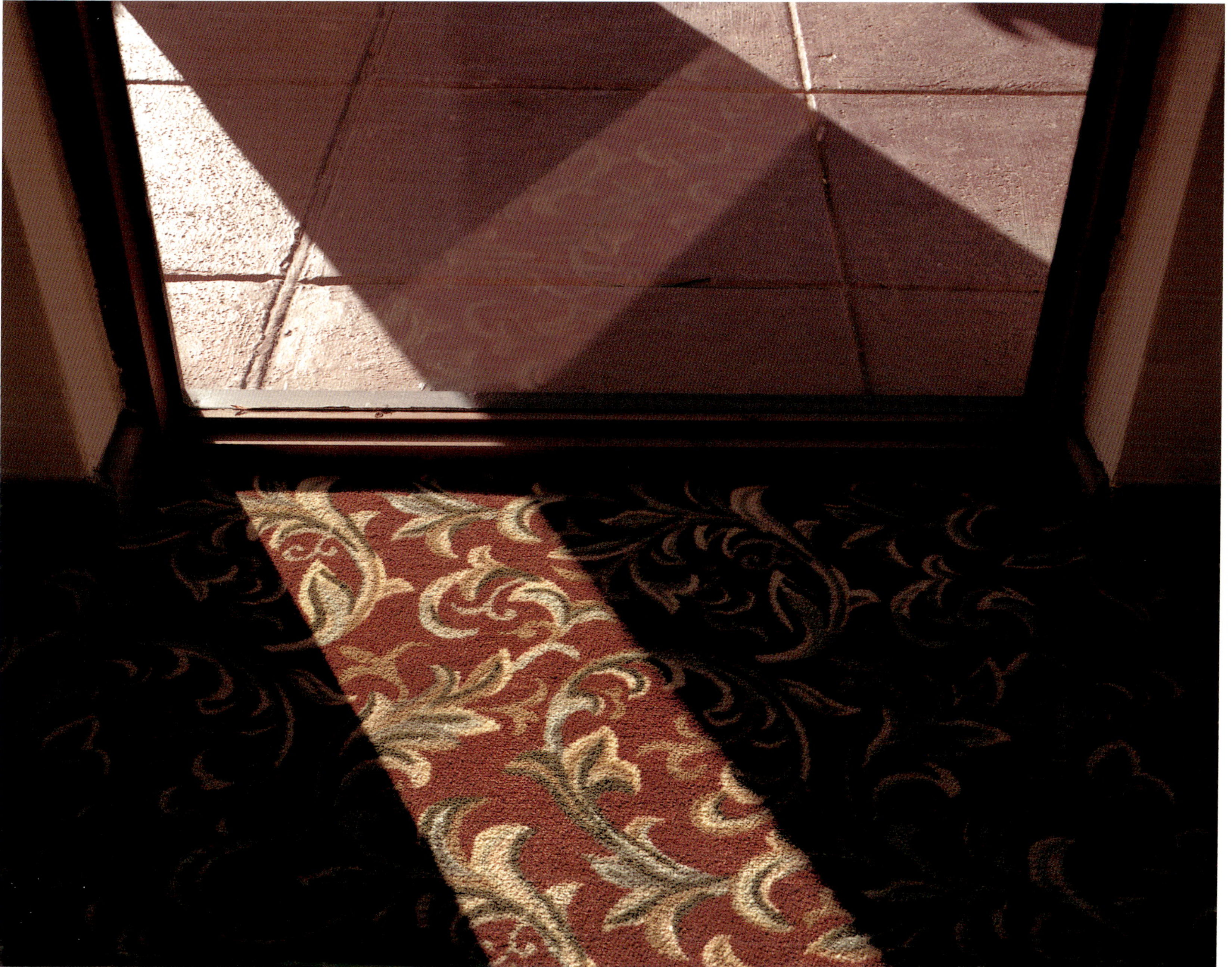

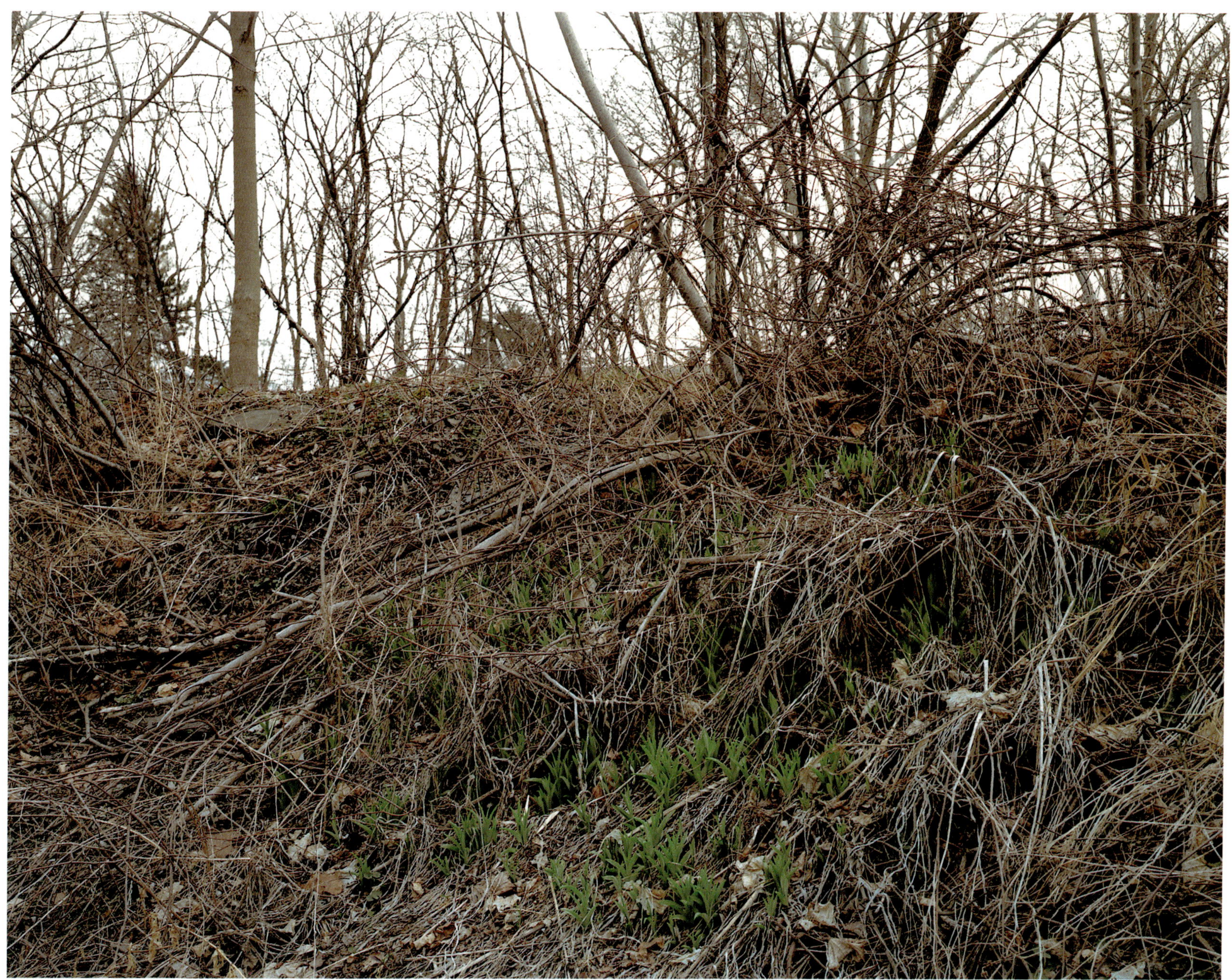

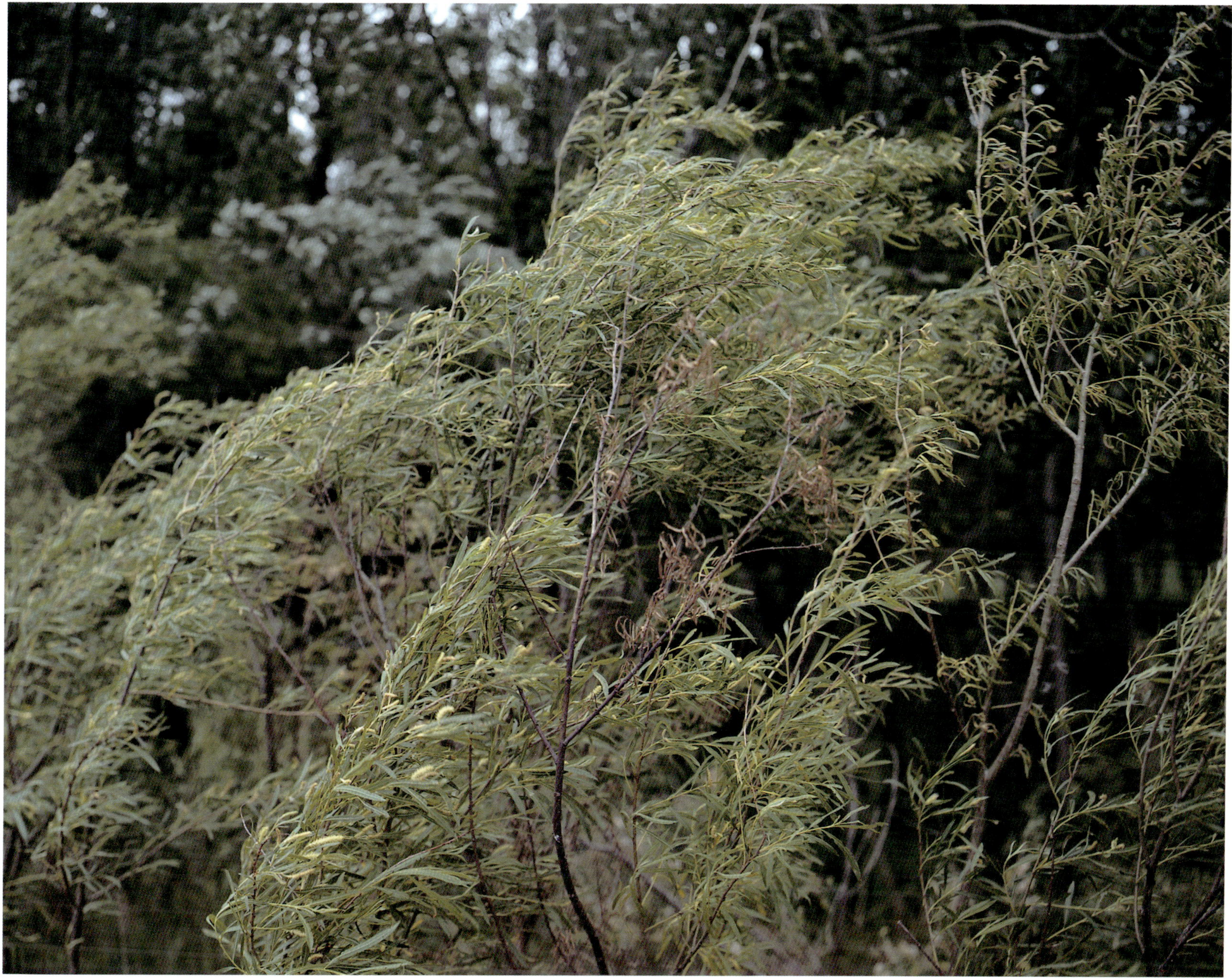

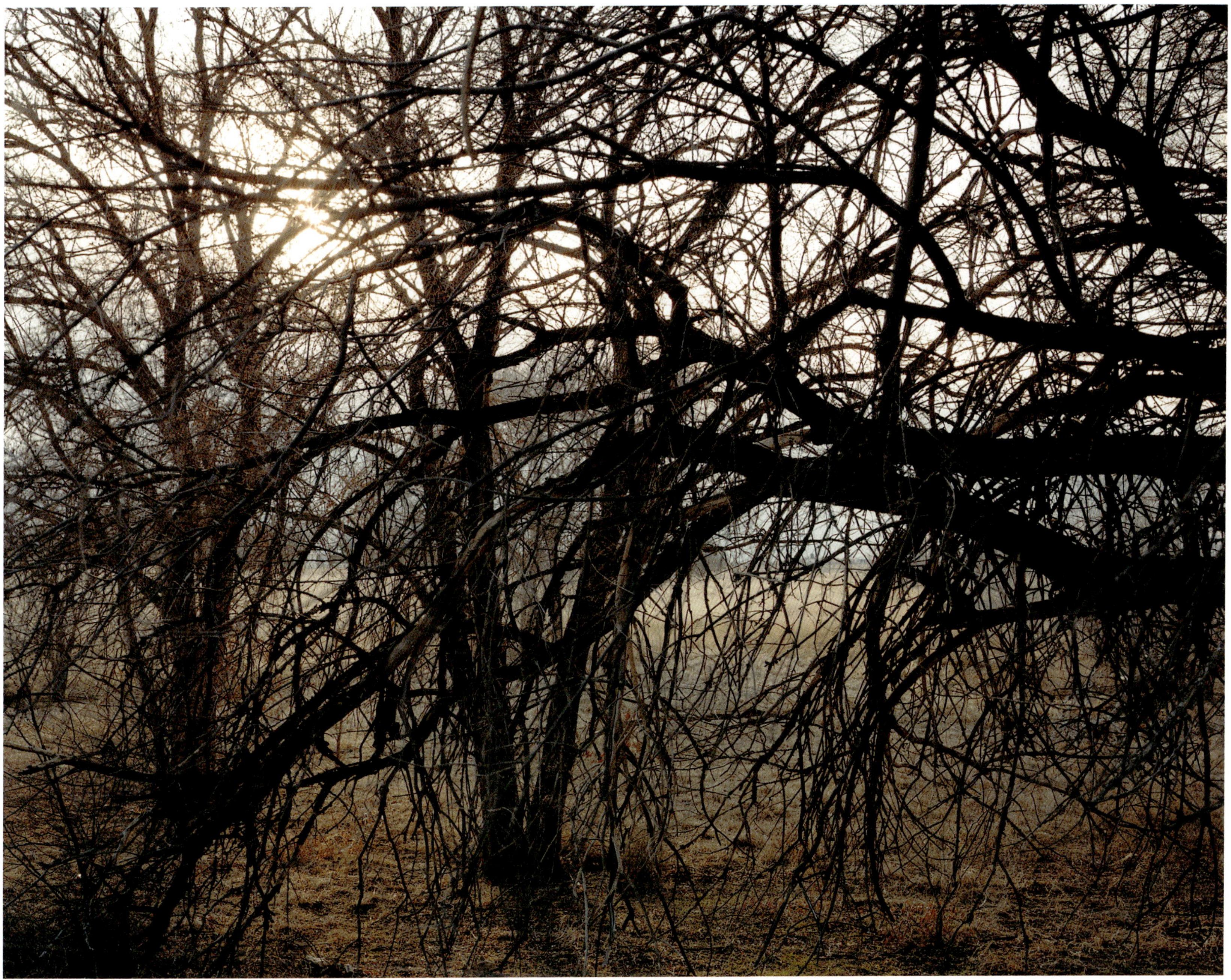

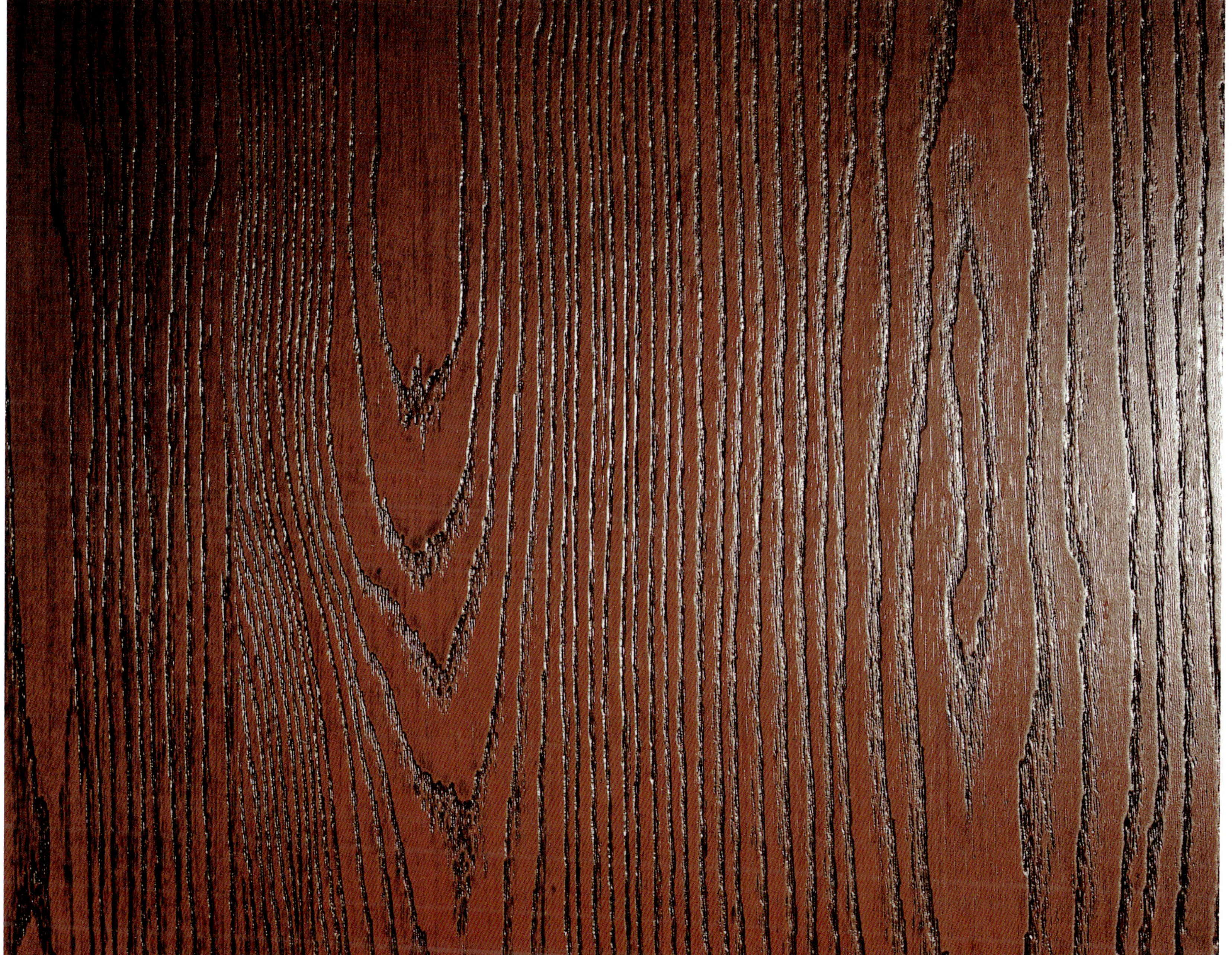

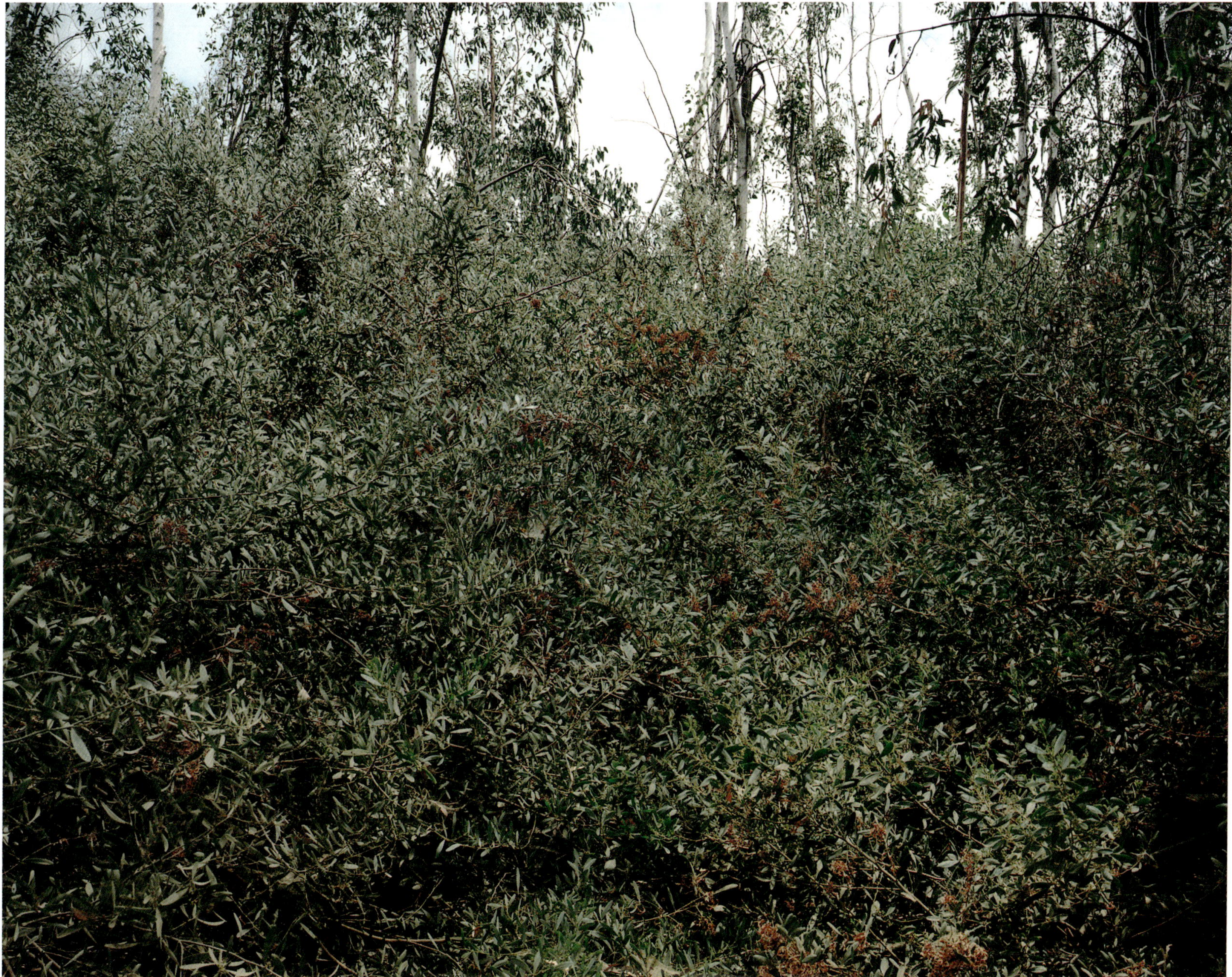

Cover: Springfield, MO
Frontispiece: San Fernando, CA

5 Los Angeles, CA
7 Baton Rouge, LA
9 Stroud, OK
11 Federal Way, WA
13 Los Angeles, CA
15 Kingman, AZ
17 Salton City, CA
19 Kingman, AZ
21 Los Angeles, CA
23 Del Rio, TX
25 Baton Rouge, LA
27 Calistoga, CA
29 Ithaca, NY
31 Ithaca, NY
33 Pasadena, CA
35 Gallup, NM
37 Seattle, WA
39 Baton Rouge, LA
41 Ithaca, NY
43 Pismo Beach, CA
45 Los Angeles, CA
47 Olympia, WA
49 Calistoga, CA
51 Santa Cruz, CA
53 Ithaca, NY
55 Tucson, AZ
57 Glendora, CA
59 Morro Bay, CA
61 Calistoga, CA
63 Lewes, DE
65 Santa Fe, NM
67 Las Cruces, NM
69 Ithaca, NY
71 Ithaca, NY
73 Marfa, TX
75 Indianapolis, IN
77 Los Angeles, CA

...When the sage says: "Go over," he does not mean that we should cross to some actual place, which we could do anyhow if the labor were worth it; he means some fabulous yonder, something unknown to us, something that he cannot designate more precisely either, and therefore cannot help us here in the very least...

—Franz Kafka, On Parables

OTHER NATURE

All photographs made by Ron Jude from 2001 to 2007

Thanks to the following for their invaluable assistance in making this project possible: Mike Slack and Tricia Gabriel; Peter Holzhauer; Dianne Lynch; Michael Book and Sarah Kracke; Wendy Mericle and Jeff Koehler; and, as always, Danielle Mericle

Travel funding provided by a James B. Pendleton Grant from the Roy H. Park School of Communications at Ithaca College

Scans: A&I, Hollywood, CA

Coordination: Jacques Marlow

Distributed in North America by D.A.P.
http://www.artbook.com

ISBN 978-0-9776481-6-0

Printed in Korea

THE ICE PLANT
P.O. Box 29247
Los Angeles, California
90029-0247 USA
http://theiceplant.cc

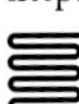